Title Page

Planning & Implementing 5S
Organizing the Workplace for Results

Brice Alvord

Limits of Liability Disclaimer of Warranty

The author and publisher of this book and the accompanying materials have used their best efforts in preparing this program. The authors and publisher make no representation or warranties with respect to (the accuracy, applicability. fitness, or completeness of the contents of this program. They disclaim any warranties expressed or implied), merchantability, or fitness for any particular purpose. The authors and publisher shall in no event beheld liable for any loss or other damages, including but not limited to special, incidental, consequential, or other damages. As always, the advice of a competent legal, tax, accounting or other professional should be sought. The author and publisher do not warrant the performance, effectiveness, or applicability of any sites listed in this book. All links are for information purposes only and are not warranted for content, accuracy or any other implied or explicit purpose.

This book contains material protected under International and Federal Copyright Laws and Treaties. Any unauthorized reprint or use of this material is prohibited.

ALERA Publishing Group
PO Box 6111
Wyomissing, PA 19610

Planning & Implementing 5S

Planning & Implementing 5S

Copyright Notice

Published by ALERA Publishing Group, Inc. Wyomissing, PA 19610

Printed in the United States of America

ISBN 978-0-557-53240-7

9 780557 532407   90000

Planning & Implementing 5S

About This Manual

Introduction

This manual is a training reference manual for helping trainees to understand advanced 5S tools and concepts. It is designed to provide clear and simple explanations of concepts, procedures and techniques that make up this program.

How To Use This Manual

There are four ways to find information in this manual:
1. The table of contents, which lists the sections of the manual
2. The table of illustrations, which lists the illustrations found in this manual
3. The section title at the top of every page which provides a quick reference as to which section the manual is open to
4. The index in the back of the book

Description

The chapters described in this manual include:
- Review of 5S Concepts
- Advanced 5S Tools
- 5S Implementation Techniques.

In This Manual

The chapters described in this manual are located as indicated below:

Topic	See Page
Understanding The Target Area	8
Organizing The Workplace	57
Planning Our Future	129

Planning & Implementing 5S

5S Program Overview

Introduction

The Planning & Implementing 5S program focuses on identifying the sources of waste in your operations, defining a waste free environment and then the methodology for eliminating that waste and keeping out of your operations.

Program Description

The Planning & Implementing 5S program shows you how to organize a Performance Improvement Steering Team (5S Team), how to analyze the workplace, how to plan a facility-wide improvement program, and how to sustain your efforts. Participants start out conducting a value-stream analysis and move on to organizing the workplace for maximum effectiveness of the people and equipment in your facility. This program is based on Hiroyuki Hirano's *5 Pillars of the Visual Workplace*; you will see the terms 5S and 3S throughout the book, these terms are synonymous with Planning & Implementing 5S

Planning & Implementing 5S

Table of Contents

Planning & Implementing 5S

Planning & Implementing 5S

Planning & Implementing 5S

Table of Figures

Table of Tables

Planning & Implementing 5S

Planning & Implementing 5S

Preparing For Your 5S Project

Overview

Introduction

There is no end to the 5S process- it is a process continually in development. 5S, like all other quality and prevention initiatives, requires commitment from top management and participation by everyone in the organization. This requires plans tailored to your facility, a 5S program cannot be implemented using a "one-size-fits-all" approach. Keep in mind, 5S is best implemented very gradually over a period of time. Since implementing five S can be such an overwhelming task, it must be instituted in target areas, department-by-department. You can not do this without proper preparation

Purpose

Make sure that your 5S activities are "successful". In other words making sure that people actually solve some of their problems using 5S principles and practices. To ensure that 5S is viewed as a part of a complete Lean initiative and not as a stand alone tool, and make sure people know why we are doing 5S.

In this Chapter

The topics described in this chapter are located as indicated below:

Topic	See Page
The Role of Management In 5S	11
Planning Your 5S Program	19

Planning & Implementing 5S

The Role of Management In 5S

Overview

Introduction This section covers the role of management in ensuring the success of the program and making sure the goals and expectations of the stakeholders are met. Management must be totally committed and involved or the program will not succeed and will become just another "flavor of the month."

Purpose To identify the roles and responsibilities of the management team with respect to the planning and implementation of the 5S program

In this Section The topics described in this section are located as indicated below

Topic	See Page
Management Commitment	13
The 5S Champion	14
5S Teams	15

Planning & Implementing 5S

Planning & Implementing 5S

Management Commitment

Introduction

Upper management's greatest role in the implementation of 5S is to communicate its commitment to a company-wide 5S implementation. Management must create a formal 5S plan and set dates for its implementation. This will require a working knowledge of 5S combined with realistic expectations for what 5S will and will not do for the company. Managers must demonstrate their commitment by:

- Active Involvement
- Ensuring Success
- Provide the necessary tools and techniques
- Enforcement of policies and procedures
- Commissioning the 5S Project.

Active Involvement

Regular oversight also is required to ensure that the processes are working as intended or changed in a controlled fashion when needed. Management must not only commit the resources, they must commit their time to get involved. They must lead from the front and have a high visibility in the workplace.

Ensuring Success

Management must refocus the workforce on a new set of measurements and processes that are focused on increasing throughput, decreasing inventory and reducing operating costs. This may mean totally abandoning many of the traditional measures like efficiency and looking more to become more effective instead.

Provide The Necessary Tools And Techniques

The management team must provide all the tools and techniques of lean manufacturing and 5S practices in order that the workers can sustain, self-audit and continuously improve the workplace and their jobs.

Enforcement of Policies And Procedures

Management must support the program with policies and procedures that are enforced.

Commissioning The 5S Project

The senior manager must write a commissioning letter or memorandum of understanding that spells out the expectations of the management team for the 5S project and defines the scope and boundaries of the project. The letter should name the 5S champion and his/her duties and the 5S Team leader. It should explain that the project team will develop certain procedures and that these will be approved and issued by management and become company policy. Finally the letter must require all managers and personnel to cooperate with the 5S project team and follow the 5S implementation plan once it is approved.

Planning & Implementing 5S

The 5S Champion

Introduction	The 5S Champion plays a critical role in the eventual success or failure of the 5S effort. Many champions make the mistake of believing that they don't need to get involved; that the project shouldn't take up too much of their time. In fact, the most successful 5S projects have champions that understand the importance of their involvement.
Role of 5S Champion	A good 5S Champion ensures that the project remains aligned to the strategic goals of the organization, and through timely involvement ensure that key decisions are made. A 5S team leader is responsible for the running of the project, but ultimately it is the 5S Champion who has more power and influence in the organization and can make things happen.
Accountability	It is the 5S Champion who is accountable for the success or failure of the project. This means that the 5S Champion will have to make the key project decisions, which are outside the approved boundaries for the 5S team. Through an effective working partnership, the 5S team leader supports the 5S Champion, ensuring he/she is aware of the key issues on the project and providing them with possible alternatives.
Communicating Business Purpose	The 5S Champion has a vital role on a 5S project and can make the difference between goals that are fully realized and goals that are only partly achieved. 5S projects need support and must be driven within an organization. Therefore, in the end, it's is up to the 5S Champion to ensure that the 5Sproject is given the management backing it needs. The 5S Champion has the important task of communicating the business purpose for the project and ensuring that the benefits are understood across the organization.

14

Planning & Implementing 5S

The 5S Team

Introduction	Getting off to a good start is half the battle for a new team. Creating a solid basis, with a clear purpose and well defined roles and expectations is a key factor in the success of any team. People generally can accomplish more working together than they can individually. This is called "synergy." Synergy means that the whole working together is greater than the sum of the individual parts working independently (1 +1 =3 or more).
Purpose	The purpose of the team approach is to provide a framework that will increase the ability of employees to participate in planning, problem solving and decision making affecting the design and implementation of the 5S program..
Need For 5S Team Approach	In order for 5Steams to fulfill their intended role of improving organizational effectiveness through 5S, it is critical that the team develops into working units that are focused on their goal, mission, or reason for existing.
5S Team Organization and Structure	The 5S team will consist of the following members: • 5S Team Leader • 5S Team Facilitator • 5S Team Recorder • 5S Team Members
Team Selection	Mistakes are often made at this point. Some companies assume it is only a production or manufacturing project and therefore do not involve any other departments, others appoint a wholly inappropriate team leader who has the company/process knowledge but not the people skills to bind others into a cross functional team.

Continued on next page

The 5S Team, Continued

5S Team Leader

The 5S Team Leader will be chosen by management prior to the commencement of 5S planning. The 5S Team Leader has the following duties:
- Assist in the initial audit and writing of the team charter
- Select the 5S team members with the guidance of the 5S Champion and management
- Ensure that a participative approach is taken to all 5S implementation
- Provide direction and support to the 5S team
- Prepare agendas and make decisions at 5S team meetings
- Obtain the resources needed by the 5S team
- Ensure that the 5S process is applied systematically
- Report to management on a regular basis.

The 5S Team Leader must be capable of operating at a cross functional level and be able to demonstrate the inter-personal skills required of a good change manager. Look for a good communicator, someone who is both persuasive and charismatic and someone who has only the best interests of the company at heart - avoid empire builders and ego trippers!

5S Team Facilitator

The 5S Team Facilitator will be chosen by the 5S Team Leader. The 5S Team Facilitator has the following duties:
- Assist in the initial audit and writing of the team charter
- Conduct 5S team meetings.
- Conduct 5S team training

5S Team Recorder

The 5S Team Recorder will be chosen by the 5S Team Leader. The 5S Team Recorder has the following duties:
- Assist in the initial audit and writing of the team charter
- Keep a written record of 5S team meetings
- Submit a recap of 5S team meetings to 5S Team Members and the 5S Team Champion.

Team Members

The 5S Team consists of 5 to 10 members selected by the 5S Team Leader and Team Champion with guidance from management. Team members are drawn from various disciplines across the facility. Approximately half should be selected from the affected target area and the other half should be knowledgeable about the processes and equipment found in the target area. This will give the team expertise and balance.

Continued on next page

The 5S Team, Continued

Team Charter

The purpose of a charter is to focus the activities and efforts on the target area. It also serves as a document for approval of the team's purpose, goals, and the roles and responsibilities of team members.

17

Planning & Implementing 5S

Planning Your 5S Program

Overview

Introduction   The biggest failure of most companies when implementing 5S is the failure to plan adequately from the start. There are two types of 5S plans:
- Overall 5S Program Plan
- Target Area Action Plans

The Overall 5S Program Plan defines the development and application of the 5S program elements across the entire facility or company. The Target Area Action Plans are short plans focused on a particular area they address:
- Action to be taken
- Who Performs it
- When it should be completed
- How it will be accomplished

Purpose   The purpose of the 5S plan is to define the project scope, critical path activities and specific tasks and responsibilities required to develop the 5S program and implement it in the various target areas across the facility.

In this Section   The topics described in this section are located as indicated below

Topic	See Page
Target Area Selection	
Planning Principles	
Scheduling Activities	

Planning & Implementing 5S

Target Area Selection

Introduction

Most organizations apply the 5S system in one area at a time rather than across and entire facility at once. The selection of a suitable target area is critical to the success of the 5S program. Choose a target to start with. Since 5S will use resources, you should begin somewhere where the payback time is shortest. Do it right so that you have a good example to set for the next target area.

Purpose

To identify an area in which to begin the implementation that will produce a quick return on investment for the resources invested.

Selection Criteria

5S will use resources, you should begin somewhere where the payback time is shortest (your target area). Do it right so that you have a good example to set for the next. Use the following criteria to select the initial target area for 5S implementation

- Select an area that has a relatively sound process and a high likelihood of success. It is important to succeed quickly in the first target area in order to build momentum for the subsequent areas
- Select an area that will be good for visibly demonstrating improvement to the rest of the organization.
- Select an area that is small and self-contained. For example, you might have unit that produces a complete product and is not dependent on other processes in the organization.

Necessary Communication

Communication with the managers of the target areas to secure their participation is crucial, because the 5S program will have a big impact on their area. This communication should include a face-to-face meeting with the appropriate managers, supervisors, and team leaders, and should cover the following issues:

- The purpose of the program
- The context in which it is being organized-who in the company is behind it, and why
- How this effort is being coordinated with other programs or
- improvement efforts in the company
- What role or responsibilities the manager has in the project.
- Planning the schedule
- Choosing the core implementation team members from inside the area as well as some who interact with the area
- An overview of the 5S System
- Any questions, concerns, or issues the managers have about the project

Continued on next page

Planning & Implementing 5S

Target Area Selection, Continued

Select The Target Area	There are two major issues to look for in the selection of a target area: • "Control issues" that are out of control • A poorly organized physical workplace
Safety Considerations	At the top of the list of control issues is safety. Any area that has a large number of safety hazards, particularly serious safety hazards, or a high accident rate, is a good candidate for the 5S program.
Defect and Error Considerations	Another indicator of a good target area is a workplace where defects and/or errors are out of control. Defects and errors are not the same. A defect is a result, whereas an error is a cause of a defect. Not all errors result in defects. Further, you can have a low defect rate due to inspection - but it would be better to prevent the error. So a high defect and/or error rate is a good indicator for a target area.
Equipment Considerations	Equipment delays or breakdowns also indicate a lack of control. Although the 5S System can't completely solve these problems, it can make serious inroads and support other companywide programs such as total productive maintenance (TPM).
Inventory Considerations	Excess inventory or supplies in an area, or delays caused by poor materials management or delivery also indicate a good target-area candidate.
Alternate Selection Method	The selection criteria mentioned to this point have been about control issues. There is method for choosing a target area. Simply observe the workplace activities in a work area, and ask yourself the following questions: • Are there too many unneeded items in the area? • Is there too much clutter? • Is there an accumulation of dirt, grime, oil, etc.? • Are items and tools difficult to find? • Is this an unpleasant place to work?

Planning & Implementing 5S

Planning Principles

Introduction

Planning requires careful and extensive research. In order to create a comprehensive 5S plan, the 5S team must:
1. Clearly define their goal in writing.
2. The goal should be "SMART"
3. Identify all the main issues which need to be addressed.
4. Review past performance.
5. Decide budgetary requirements.
6. Focus on business needs.
7. Define Target Area requirements and how will they be met?
8. Decide on the probable length of the plan and its structure?
9. Identify shortcomings in the concept and gaps.
10. Describe strategies for implementation.

Purpose

The plan serves the following three critical functions:
- Helps management to clarify, focus
- Provides a considered and logical framework for the 5S program
- Presents a benchmark against which actual performance can be measured and reviewed.

Clearly Define The Goal

Setting goals is an important part of your journey to success. What happens if you don't set goals?
- How do you know where you are headed?
- How do you know if you are succeeding at your job?
- How will you prioritize your daily tasks?
- How will you feel a sense of accomplishment?

Properly defining your goals makes your job easier and more manageable. Goals must be defined in terms of the SMART Characteristics listed below.

"SMART" Goals

S.M.A.R.T. Goals set you up for success; they have five characteristics that create the best chances for achieving the goal. They must be:
- Specific
- Measurable
- Agreed upon
- Realistic
- Time based

Continued on next page

Planning & Implementing 5S

Planning Principles, Continued

Identify Main Issues	The next step in planning effectively is to identify all the main issues which need to be addressed. The project scope is defined in terms of the issues facing the 5S team and the appropriate methods for completing the project are determined.
Review Past Performance	Once you have identified the main issues, it is important to go back and review them in terms of past performance. You will want to make a note of both positive and negative past performance and describe each issue and the contributing factor or root cause of each.
Decide Budgetary Requirements	At this point the idea is not to develop a complete budget fo implementation, but rather develop the high level budgetary requirements for planning and Implementing the 5S project. These are your project goal posts.
Focus On Business Needs	When determining your budgetary requirement, keep them focused in terms of business needs. Strategic thinking will help you in this effort.
Define Target Area Requirements	What are the requirements for your target area? These requirements should address all five areas of the 5S program. Your Target Area requirements become your Work Breakdown structure and allow you to identify the logical dependencies between tasks. Create an activity network diagram that enables identification of the critical path.
Decide Probable Length And Structure	In order to complete your network diagram (or schedule) requires that you make an estimate of the length of time or duration of each of tasks in your work breakdown structure.
Identify Shortcomings And Gaps	The 5S project team should review the schedule developed above in order to identify issues, shortcomings and gaps that will impact the success of the project. Each of these should be documented and addressed using problems solving techniques.
Describe Strategies For Implementation	One you have identified the task steps and any issues, shortcomings and gaps, the team must devise strategies for implementation of the project elements. These strategies should be documented using a 5S plan document as shown in the Appendix on page 154

Planning & Implementing 5S

Scheduling 5S Activities

Introduction

Project scheduling is concerned with the techniques that can be employed to manage the activities that need to be undertaken during the development of the 5S project. Scheduling is carried out in advance of the project start up and involves:

- Identifying the tasks that need to be carried out (Work breakdown structure)
- Estimating how long they will take
- Allocating resources (mainly personnel)
- Scheduling when the tasks will occur.

Purpose

The purpose of scheduling is to provide a "roadmap" that represents how and when the project will deliver the products defined in the project scope and by the project team.

Schedule Development

Developing a schedule means determining planned start-and-finish dates for each activity. After you have identified project activities and established how long each should take, it is possible to connect them to actual calendar dates. These may then be displayed as:

- Gantt charts
- Network diagrams
- Milestone charts.

Figure 1: Typical Schedule

ID	Task Name	Start	End	Duration	Jun 2000								Jul 2000					
					23	24	25	26	27	28	29	30	1	2	3	4	5	6
1	Task 1	6/23/00	6/23/00	1 d														
2	Task 2	6/26/00	6/28/00	3 d														
3	Milestone 1	6/29/00	6/29/00	0 d														
4	Task 3	6/29/00	6/30/00	2 d														
5	Task 4	6/30/00	7/4/00	3 d														
6	Task 5	7/3/00	7/4/00	2 d														
7	Milestone 2	7/5/00	7/5/00	0 d														

Gantt Chart

A Gantt chart is a graphic display of schedule-related information. In the typical Gantt chart, activities are listed down the left side of the chart, dates are shown across the top or bottom, and planned activity duration is shown as a horizontal bar, placed according to the dates. A Gantt chart is sometimes called a "bar chart."

Continued on next page

Planning & Implementing 5S

Scheduling 5S Activities, Continued

Purpose

Because the Gantt bars are proportionally longer for project activities that take longer to complete, Gantt charts can effectively display relative differences in duration of activities.

When to Use

Choose a Gantt chart when you want to show which activities will take longer than others. Note that project management software packages create high-quality Gantt charts quickly and easily. A sample of a Gantt chart is shown below.

Figure 2: Simple Gantt Chart

ID	Task Name	Start	End	Duration	Jun 2009										Jul 2009			
					21	22	23	24	25	26	27	28	29	30	1	2	3	4
1	Conduct 5C Analysis	6/21/00	6/21/00	4h														
2	Conduct SWOT Analysis	6/22/00	6/22/00	1d														
3	Develop Conclusions & Implications	6/23/00	6/23/00	1d														
4	Develop Goals	6/26/00	6/26/00	1d														
5	Develop Strategy	6/27/00	6/28/00	2d														
6	Develop Guaging Impact Measures	7/3/00	7/4/00	2d														

NEST Process

Network Diagrams

In scheduling tasks, we often find that a given task cannot begin until other tasks have been completed. What network diagrams do is incorporate scheduling information into a basic flow chart diagram. There are two types of network diagrams:
- Arrow
- Precedence diagram.

Purpose

A network diagram, as shown in Figure 3, shows which project activities depend on which other activities in order to be completed. Choose a network diagram when you want to clearly show the relationships among activities.

Continued on next page

26

Scheduling 5S Activities, Continued

Figure 3: Typical Network Diagram

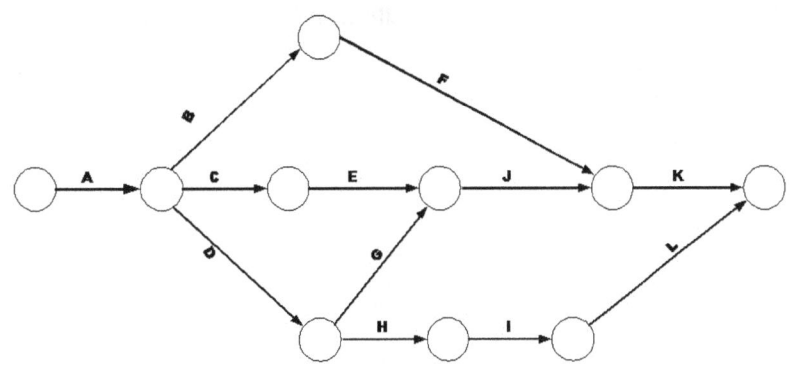

Milestone Charts   Milestone charts show only the most significant project events.

Purpose   Choose a milestone chart when you want to provide broad overviews of the project's main events for executive audiences or others who want to see only the big picture?

Figure 4: Simple Milestone Chart

ID	Task Name	End	Duration	Jun 2000								Jul 2000												
				22	23	24	25	26	27	28	29	30	1	2	3	4	5	6	7	8	9	10	11	12	13
1	Planning & Situational Analysis completed	6/26/00	0w				◆																	
2	Consumer Needs & Idea Generation completed	6/27/00	0w						◆															
3	Concept Development completed	6/30/00	0w								◆													
4	Product Development completed	7/4/00	0w											◆										
5	Product Launch completed	7/7/00	0w													◆								
6	Post-Launch Audit completed	7/12/00	0w																		◆		

Product Development Process Milestone Chart

Continued on next page

Scheduling 5S Activities, Continued

Scheduling Procedure

Use the following procedure to develop a project schedule:

Step	Action
1	Assemble the following: • Your estimates of duration and resources required • Information about availability of resources--how many will be available and when • Organization calendars--these identify when work is allowed (when resources w/ll be available, which days are holidays, which days are vacation days, and so on). • Project constraints, including: • Imposed dates based on stakeholder requirements, seasonal weather, and so forth • Key events or major milestone completion dates • Unusual assumptions about resources or durations • A blank calendar or other blank form on which to record the schedule.
2	On the blank calendar, label any holidays or other dates when resources won't be available. • Identify holidays, vacations, and the like.
3	Examine each activity and its duration, and plot the activity on the calendar. On a separate page labeled "Assumptions," capture any assumptions about the activity, including assumptions about the resources to be assigned. • Plot activities, durations • List assumptions about resources.
4	After the days are plotted on a standard calendar, create other types of schedule displays that will be useful (e.g., Gantt charts, network diagrams, milestone charts, text tables). Create specialized project-wide charts, schedules.

Continued on next page

Scheduling 5S Activities, Continued

Scheduling Procedure (continued)

Step	Action
5	If your project's network diagram or Gantt chart shows many different activities happening at the same time, consider finding the critical path and attempting to shorten it in order to reduce the project's overall duration. (The critical path is that sequence of activities that takes the most time to complete.)
	Here are some ways you can shorten the critical path:
	• Reduce the duration of some of the activities. (Simply allow less time for them.)
	• Add more resources to some of the activities. (If you assign more people or equipment, you can often reduce the time required. Be careful, however, since this can increase the coordination time required.)
	• Allow more hours in the workday. (Allow for overtime or add another shift.); Allow more workdays in the schedule. (Allow for weekend or holiday work.)
	• Change the relationships of activities. (Instead of performing some tasks sequentially, one at a time, perform them at the same time, in parallel fashion.)
	• Use slack time more effectively. (Find slack between activities or "downtime" for some resources, and "move up" or plan to complete pending activities during this time.)
	• Redefine one or more project phases. (Check to see if some activities contained within a phase are causing the phase to be delayed needlessly; then consider moving these activities to the next phase.)
	• Reduce the amount of deliverables that a particular activity produces. (It takes less time to do less work!)
	• Reduce the overall project scope. (Eliminate some work products, processes, or deliverables.)

Continued on next page

Scheduling 5S Activities, Continued

Caution:	After you have determined which of the methods you would like to use to shorten the critical path, you should discuss them with your sponsors or stakeholders. Since many of these methods result in fundamental changes in project structure, you should discuss the positive and negative effects they might have on the project, and obtain sponsor/stakeholder approval.

Planning & Implementing 5S

Understanding The Target Area

Overview

Introduction	This chapter provides the preliminary information and skills necessary to understand the current workplace and to decide upon improvement activities.
Purpose	The purpose of understanding the target area is to make it easier for the 5S team to identify 5S targets and design a program for applying the principles and practices of 5S to the workplace and to implement the program successfully
In this Chapter	The topics described in this chapter are located as indicated below:

Topic	See Page
Planning & Implementing 5S	32
Workplace Analysis	48

Planning & Implementing 5S

Planning & Implementing 5S

Overview

Introduction	This section is intended to provide the participant with a foundation knowledge of Planning & Implementing 5S.
Purpose	Planning & Implementing 5S fundamentals are important for the participant to understand. They form the basis upon which the activities in following sections are built.
In this Section	The topics described in this section are located as indicated below

Topic	See Page
Explain Waste	33
Explain Value Stream Analysis	40
Describe The Fundamentals of 5S	46

32

Planning & Implementing 5S

Concepts of Waste In Operations

Introduction   This unit introduces the participant to the terminology and concepts of waste in operations.

Definition   Waste is defined as: *using something carelessly*: to use something or use something up carelessly, extravagantly, or without effect; or *failing to use something*: to fail to make use of something such as an opportunity, or *unwanted material*: unwanted or unusable by-products.

Purpose   The purpose of understanding waste is to be able to identify it in its many forms and to devise means of reducing its impact on operations.

Continued on next page

Planning & Implementing 5S

Concepts of Waste In Operations, Continued

Table 1:Types of Waste Affecting Operations Performance

The following types of waste affect operations performance":

Type of Waste	Description
WASTE OF CAPITAL	
Financial Arrangements	Financial arrangements such as selling of stock at the wrong time, purchasing decisions with bad timing, borrowing at other than the optimal rates and terms, debentures offered at the wrong time or terms, mergers and acquisitions done for the wrong reasons, and other financial moves may be a source of wasted capital. Too often, such moves are made in support of short-term goals that are contrary to the long-term interest of the organization.
Inventory	A lot of companies practice "just-in-case" inventory, when they should be working toward "just-in-time" inventory. Rather than have an extra week or month of inventory because it's comfortable and something might go wrong, companies need to rid themselves of potential problems that require "safety" stocks.
Receivables	A major challenge facing companies today is getting paid on time for products or services delivered. Companies with a high percentage of late receivables often blame the customer. Yet late receivables are almost invariably due to errors the supplier has made. To find the waste in receivables, it's important to understand the process, to learn what percentage of receivables is late and why. Often receivables are late because of billing mistakes, or because the invoice was sent to the wrong address, or because of similar kinds of mix-ups. Once the reasons are uncovered, take steps to eliminate the problems and get everyone doing their jobs right the first time.

Continued on next page

Planning & Implementing 5S

Concepts of Waste In Operations, Continued

Table 1:Types of Waste Affecting Operations Performance (continued)

Type of Waste	Description
WASTE OF CAPITAL	
Equipment	Unnecessary or excess equipment that's not utilized fully is a waste of capital. For example, back-up equipment is often a form of waste. A $2 million piece of equipment should not be purchased with the expectation that it will break down. Rather than waste money on extra equipment as back-up, take steps to ensure that the main piece of equipment isn't likely to malfunction, and that it can be quickly repaired if it does.
Excessive Cost of Goods	Excess costs are not always due to supplier over-charges. An organization has to look at the real price or value of materials and/or services. The real price or value goes beyond the purchase price. The quality and reliability of materials purchased, as well as the relationship established with the supplier, determine the true cost of goods in terms of defects, rework, availability issues, etc. The absolute lowest-priced supplier may not be the lowest-cost supplier. Capital is wasted if a supplier is providing poor quality or inconsistent quality goods, even if they are offered at a competitive or low price.
Capacity	Corporations often decide to build new plants and buy new equipment when their current plants and machines aren't at or near capacity. The time that equipment is not being used to manufacture products can be classified as waste. Oversized boilers, extra power supplies, and back-ups for other central services are also potential forms of waste unless they are part of well-thought-out long-range plans

Continued on next page

Concepts of Waste In Operations, Continued

Table 1:Types of Waste Affecting Operations Performance (continued)

Type of Waste	Description
Interest Payments	A significant portion of interest payments can also be a form of waste. By freeing capital tied up in excess inventory and late receivables, a company can substantially reduce its need to borrow money.
WASTE OF MATERIAL	
Scrap	The most visible type of wasted material is scrap. People see it in trash cans, in trucks hauling waste to the dump. This form of waste has probably received the most attention because it is the most obvious indicator of poor quality production.
Seconds	In some cases seconds are sold by cutting the price, so this may not seem like waste. But it's a very costly form of waste. The waste is the difference between the original selling price of the product and the price it must be marked down to because of a mistake. In addition, companies that sell seconds often become "second-rate" suppliers in the eyes of their customers, so this form of waste might also result in waste from lost sales if customers turn elsewhere for quality products.
Energy	Waste can result from the amount and kind of energy used. Plant locations can lead to waste if freight and distribution costs are higher than they need to be.

Continued on next page

Concepts of Waste In Operations, Continued

Table 1:Types of Waste Affecting Operations Performance (continued)

Type of Waste	Description
Variability In Materials	Variation points people to problems in systems and processes. When materials are used that vary in attributes, the end-product will not be consistent and the result is waste. Variation from sample to sample or shipment to shipment makes it difficult to produce consistently high quality and to maintain high productivity. An organization pays for waste in the supplier's systems and processes in more than one way. The quality and productivity deficiencies are imported into the customer's systems and processes. The result is a "ripple effect" whereby the deficiencies are magnified at each level of assembly and use. This ripple effect can be as great as 10-to-1 at each level.
WASTE OF TIME	
Improper Training & Development of Human Talent	The selection of training which does not contribute to the improvement of a job or process or lead to continuous improvement wastes people's time. When people or machines or computers spend time on programs that contribute little or nothing to increasing quality and productivity, it's an expensive waste of time--time that could and should have been spent working on other things.
Poor Work Methods	Even when people are working on the right things at the right time, poor work methods can be a major cause of lost productivity and poor quality. The improvement of all processes and work events that compose the processes is paramount. Wasteful motion, unnecessary steps, waiting time, and inappropriate working pace, all contribute to costly wastes of time.

Continued on next page

Concepts of Waste In Operations, Continued

Table 1: Types of Waste Affecting Operations Performance (continued)

Type of Waste	Description
Poor Human Relations	When a human relations system isn't effective, people simply don't use their time as well as they could. If they are working in a negative or stifling atmosphere where labor-management relations are strained, they cannot give 100%. When management creates an atmosphere of tension and fear for people at all levels, productivity will fall and quality will suffer because fear does not encourage the sharing of ideas or the cooperation of the people doing the work.
WASTE FROM LOST SALES & OPPORTUNITIES	
Market Timing Problems	Entering the wrong market or entering at the wrong time is a major cause of waste from sales that could have been made but weren't. A company may move too late to take advantage of a lucrative market opportunity. By the time the product is ready or the public is aware of it, the market may be overcrowded or the product's technology or appeal might be passé
Market Definition Problems	Sales and marketing efforts must be well targeted and focused. If markets are not clearly defined, advertising, promotional, and direct sales efforts will not easily reach likely buyers. The full researching and clear definition of the nature and makeup of the market for any product or service are central to avoiding waste of capital, time and lost sales.
Product Problems	Such problems as poor product quality, unreliability, inadequate or inappropriate features, and unacceptable delivery schedules lead to lost sales. Unless an organization provides customers with the products or services the customer wants, when and where the customer wants them, sales will be lost.

Continued on next page

Concepts of Waste In Operations, Continued

Table 1:Types of Waste Affecting Operations Performance (continued)

Type of Waste	Description
Inadequate Capacity	Sales will also be lost if the product satisfies external customers' requirements but is not available in the quantities that customers need. Organizations must be able to make what customers want when they want it.
WASTE FROM LOST SALES & OPPORTUNITIES	
Sales & Marketing Performance Problems	Sales will be lost if sales people are not calling on the right customers or if they are spending time on rework or unnecessary work rather than on the real (value added) work needed to make the sales.
Pricing Problems	The wrong pricing strategy can cause waste regardless of whether the price is set too high or too low. If too high, the pricing strategy will lead to lost sales through undercutting by the competition. If too low, the organization is losing profits that could be achieved without affecting sales volume. An organization' s pricing strategy can also result in waste if products within a product line cause confusion, and overlapping price/performance causes indecision for the customer or sales force.
Customer Support Problems	Insufficient or wrongly priced customer support for products and services is a prominent cause of waste. Although hard to quantify, a lack of good field service and support can lead to customer ill will and frustration--and a loss of resale opportunities, if not the loss of the account itself. It also wastes the time of sales resources who try to fix problems and soothe angry customers.

Value Stream Analysis

Introduction

This unit introduces the participant to the terminology and concepts of Value Stream Analysis

Definition

A value stream is all of the actions (both value added and non-value added) currently required to bring a product through the main flows essential to every product.

Purpose

The purpose of the Value Stream Analysis is to highlight sources of waste and eliminate them by implementing a future state value stream that can become a reality within a short period of time.

Figure 5: Value Stream Improvement

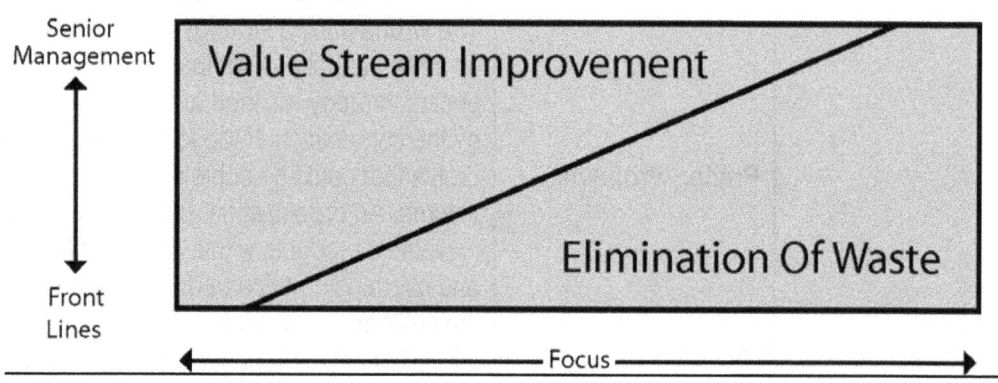

Continued on next page

Value Stream Analysis, Continued

Terms and Definitions

The following terms and definitions are critical to Value Stream Analysis.

Term	Definition
Value Stream	A value stream is all of the actions (both value added and non-value added) currently required to bring a product through the main flows essential to every product
Current State Map	A current state map is a set of symbols arranged to show the flow of product through the systems as it exists at present.
Future State Map	The future state map is a set of symbols arranged to show the flow of product through the systems as it should exist with all of the waste eliminated.

Value Stream Mapping Tools

Introduction	This unit explains the use of value stream mapping tools to create either a current state or future state map.
Description	The icons and symbols which make up the value stream mapping tools fall into three categories: • Material Flow • Information • General Icons.
Purpose	The value stream mapping tools are used to represent processes and flows.

Continued on next page

Planning & Implementing 5S

Value Stream Mapping Tools, Continued

Figure 6: Value Stream Mapping Symbols

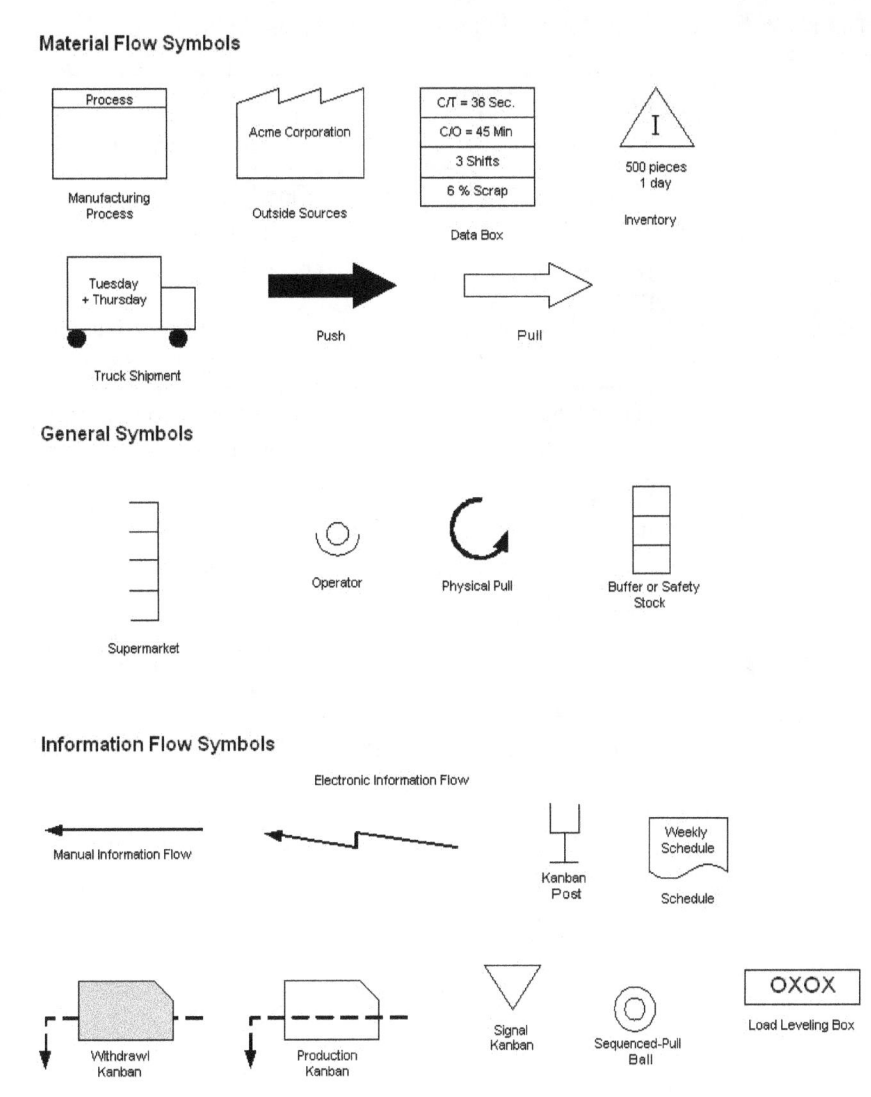

Continued on next page

Value Stream Mapping Tools, Continued

Map Icons & Symbols

The icons in Figure 6 are explained in the table below:

Icon	Notes
Material Icons	
Manufacturing Process	One box equals an area of continuous flow. All processes should be labeled. The box is also used for departments.
Outside Sources	Used to show customers, suppliers, and outside manufacturing processes.
Data Box	Used to record information concerning a manufacturing process, departments, etc.
Inventory	Count and time should be noted.
Truck Shipment	Note frequency of shipments.
Push Arrow	Identifies material movements that are pushed by producer, not pulled by the customer (following process).
Pull Arrow	Identifies material movements that are pulled by the customer, not pushed by producer.
Supermarket	Holding area from which product can be pulled as needed by the downstream process.
Physical Pull	Pull of materials from the supermarket.

Continued on next page

Value Stream Mapping Tools, Continued

Map Icons & Symbols (continued)

Icon	Notes
General Symbols	
Buffer or Safety Stock	"Buffer" or "Safety Stock" must be noted.
Operator	Represents a person viewed from above.
Information Icons	
Manual Information Flow	For example: • Production schedule • Shipping schedule.
Electronic Information Flow	Foe example, via EDI.
Information Icons	
Schedule	Describes an information flow.
Production Kanban	Tells a process how many of what can be produced and gives permission to do so.
Withdrawal Kanban	Tells how many of what can be withdrawn and gives permission to do so.
Signal Kanban	Kanban used with batch processes that signal when a reorder point has been reached and another batch needs to be produced.
Kanban Post	Place where Kanban are collected and held for conveyance.
Load leveling	Tool to level the volume over a specified period of time.
Sequenced-Pull Ball	Gives permission to produce a predetermined type and quantity.

45

Planning & Implementing 5S

The Fundamentals of 5S

Introduction

This unit introduces the participant to the terminology and concepts of Planning & Implementing 5S

Definition

Planning & Implementing 5S is based on the Japanese concept of 5S as presented by Hiroyuki Hirano in his book 5 Pillars Of The Visual Workplace. The five pillars are:
1. **Seri** – Organization
2. **Seiton** – Orderliness
3. **Seiso** – Cleanliness
4. **Seiketsu** – Standardized Clean up
5. **Shitsuke** – Discipline.

Purpose

The concepts presented above form the support system upon which effective performance improvement activities are based. This support system (5 pillars) must become a part of the plant culture if improvement programs are to become something more than "the flavor-of-the-month."

Figure 7: 5S System

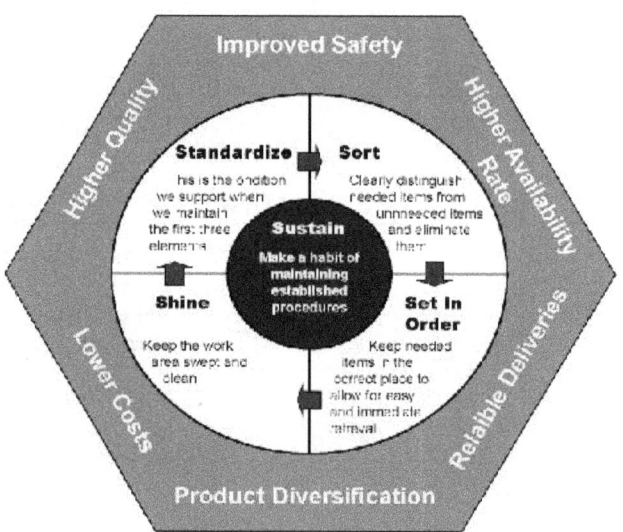

Continued on next page

The Fundamentals of 5S, Continued

Terms and Definitions

The following terms and definitions are critical to 5S:

Term	Definition
Sort	Sort means that you remove all items from the workplace that are not needed for current production operations. Many workplaces are filled with a clutter of tools, papers, product, broken items, etc. – a hodgepodge of useful items and things kept around without a good reason. This mess makes it hard to put your hands on the things you really need to do your work.
Set In Order	Set In Order means that you find the best way to store items so that you always know where they are and so that you can find them easily.
Shine	Shine means sweeping floors, wiping off equipment, and generally making sure that everything in the workplace stays clean. This component of the 5S program emphasizes the removal of dirt, grime, debris, and dust from the workplace.
Standardize	Standardize differs from Sort, Set In Order, and Shine, all of which are activities. In contrast, Standardize is the result of continuous maintenance of the first three activities (sometimes known as 3S). Standardize means finding ways to make the 3S activities into a habit.
Sustain	Sustain is the discipline or set of approaches that make people want to keep applying best practice in shop organization and housekeeping. In this sense, discipline is perhaps an unfortunate term as it implies people forced to do something, with consequent penalties if they do not.

Planning & Implementing 5S

Workplace Analysis

Overview

Introduction	This section shows the participant how to conduct a Workplace Analysis
Purpose	The Workplace Analysis is the foundation of the Planning & Implementing 5S program. Its purpose is for you to clearly understand the current condition of your work area so that you can establish a vision of what you want it to look like and to identify opportunities for improvement.
In this Section	The topics described in this section are located as indicated below:

Topic	See Page
Establish The Current State Map	49
Create the VFA Problem Chart	51
Prepare a VFA Feedback Chart.	52
Create the Future State Map	55

Planning & Implementing 5S

Establish the Current State Map

Introduction

This unit shows the participant how to establish a Current State Map.

Description

Mapping begins at the "Door-to-Door" level in your plant where you draw process categories like: mixing, machining, baking, packaging instead of recording each process step. You can change the level of magnification and zoom in to map every individual step in each category, or zoom out to encompass the value stream external to your plant.

Purpose

The purpose of the current state map is to show you the overall flow through the plant. The point is not the map, but to understand the flow of information and material.

Procedure

Use the following procedure develop a current state map:

Step	Action
Developing Flow Diagram	
1	Collect current – state information while walking along the actual pathways of material and information flows yourself.
2	Start at the end of the process (not the beginning) and work up stream. This way you will begin with the processes linked most directly to the customer. Use a stop watch to determine actual times – do not rely on standard time or information that you do not personally obtain.
3	Use a Yellow Post-It Note to identify each part of the process. Write the name and/or draw the symbol on the post-it note and attach it to the paper on the wall.
4	Continue to the previous step in the flow (remember, you are working backwards.
5	Do these steps until you have the entire flow diagrammed?

Continued on next page

Establish the Current State Map, Continued

Procedure (continued)

Step	Action
	Data Gathering
6	Go out to the target area and look for amounts of inventory, waste, unsafe conditions, and other problems.
7	Observe each step of the process to determine the amount of product flow and time to produce it.
8	Indicate the amount of inventory on a yellow Post-It™.
9	Write in the amounts and time on a yellow Post-It note with a data box drawn on it. Place it below the appropriate symbol in your flow diagram.
10	Using a post-it of a different color, identify examples of waste and place the post-it beneath the appropriate symbol.
11	Check you current-state map against the actual area to ensure its accuracy.
	Gather Information Flow Data
12	Go back to the target area and determine how information flows to each step of your flow diagram.
13	Using a different color Post-It note, diagram the flow of information from the end of the current-state map.
14	Verify the correctness of the information.
15	Your current-state map is now complete.

Planning & Implementing 5S

Create the VFA Problem Chart

Introduction

There are four steps in the process to Create the VFA Problem Charts through a process called Visual Feedback Photography

- Taking photographs of workplace problem areas

- Returning at set intervals to take a new round of pictures of the same areas

- Focusing the camera on the same targets in each round of photographs

- Shooting each round of photographs with the camera in the same position (same height, angle, and distance from each target).

Purpose

The VFA Problem Chart is a means of capturing opportunities for improvement in the workplace using photographs to inform and inspire team-based workplace improvement activities.

Continued on next page

Create the VFA Problem Chart, Continued

Procedure

Use the following procedure to develop an VFA Problem Chart:

Step	Action
1	Inspect the Current State Map and make a list of potential target areas, such as messy or potentially dangerous areas that could be improved.
2	Working with this list, choose subjects for the VFA Problem Chart.
3	One team member takes a picture of each subject.
4	.As each area is photographed, team members mark the position of the photographer's feet on the floor and note the camera position and focus relative to the subject.
5	Make a numbered list is of each picture using an OP log sheet.
6	Organize these initial photos and attach them to a VFA Problem Chart.
7	Print three copies of each picture and used as follows: • One copy is stored in an archive • A second copy is attached directly to the VFA Problem Chart • The third copy is used on the VFA Feedback Chart..
8	Use transparent tape or push pins to attach the VFA Problem chart to a stiff display board.
9	Place the VFA Problem Chart in a designated area where the team meets.

Planning & Implementing 5S

Prepare a VFA Feedback Chart.

Introduction	This unit explains the process for creating a VFA Feedback Chart.
Purpose	The VFA Feedback Chart. has two goals: • To make photographic records of current conditions • To take time lapse series of photographs of the same target location.
Record Conditions that are Hard to Quantify	Disorderly mounds of materials and dirt are hard to quantify. Different people have different rating scales and what may look good to one person, may look marginal or unsatisfactory to another. Photos capture the conditions as they were at the time of the photo, allowing people to make their own assessment at a later date.
Recognition of Subtle Changes	Often improvements consist of a series of small changes that are important but hard to see. A series of photographs mounted on a VFA Feedback Chart. helps pinpoint subtle changes that might otherwise be difficult to recognize.

Continued on next page

Planning & Implementing 5S

Prepare a VFA Feedback Chart., Continued

Procedure   Use the following procedure to create and maintain a VFA Feedback Chart.

Step	Action
	Initial Preparation
1	Prepare supplies.
2	Select photos from the VFA Problem Chart as indicated in step 7 of the VFA Problem Chart procedure.
3	Glue one set of each photo in the round 1 column of your chart.
4	Label the picture and supply information on location, date, target owner, etc.
5	Display the chart.
	Adding Photos
6	Take a second round of photos, using the VFP log to make sure that pictures are taken from the same location and point of view. Take several shots of each target.
7	Review the pictures as a team and select best pictures to represent each target.
8	Attach the new picture in the second round column.
9	Re-display the VFA Feedback Chart.
10	Follow steps 6 – 10 for rounds 3 and 4. If a target improvement is completed before round 4 take a final picture of the improved target and make a notation in the next available column, in the spot where the picture would normally go.

Planning & Implementing 5S

Create the Future State Map

Introduction

This unit shows the participant how to create a Future State Map.

Description

The future state map is similar to the current state map; it also begins at the end of the process and works backwards. The difference between the two is that you have removed most or all of the waste.

Purpose

The purpose of a future state map is to build a chain of production where individual processes are linked to their customer(s) either by a continuous flow or pull, and each process gets a close as possible to producing only what its customer(s) need when they need it.

Procedure

Use the following procedure to create a Future State Map

Step	Action
	Demand
1	Determine Takt Time for downstream processes.
2	Determine if you need to build a finished goods supermarket from which the customer pulls, or direct to shipping.
	Material Flow
3	Determine where you can use continuous flow processing.
4	Identify where you will need to use supermarket pull systems to control production of upstream processes.
	Information Flow
5	Determine at what point in the production chain you will schedule production. Keep in mind that all material transfers downstream of the pacemaker process need to occur as a flow.
6	Determine how to level production mix at the pacemaker process.
7	Determine the increment of work you will consistently release and takeaway at the pacemaker process.

Continued on next page

55

Create the Future State Map, Continued

Procedure (continued)

Step	Action
	Supporting Improvements
8	Determine the process improvements that will be necessary for the value stream to flow as the future state design specifies.
9	Starting at the end of your new process, diagram the process flow.

Planning & Implementing 5S

Creating the 5S System

Overview

Introduction

This chapter provides the information necessary for the participant to be able to improve the workplace.

Purpose

The purpose of organizing the workplace is to help participants identify the sources of waste in operations, defining a waste free environment and then the methodology for eliminating that waste and keeping out of the operations.

In this Chapter

The topics described in this chapter are located as indicated below:

Topic	See Page
Sort	57
Set-In Order	71
Shine	85
Standardize	99
Sustain	113

57

Planning & Implementing 5S

Sort

Overview

Introduction

This section describes the methodology for sort.

Description

Sort begins by figuring out what you really don't need to have around. This is accomplished using the red-tagging method. People inspect their own workplace and place a red-tag on every item that doesn't really need to be there.

Purpose

The purpose of Sort is to remove from the workplace, items that are not needed to support current production or operations.

Procedure

Use the following procedure to implement the Red-Tag method:

Step	Action
1	Launch the red tagging project
2	Identify red-tag targets
3	Set red-tag criteria
4	Make red-tags
5	Attach red-tags
6	Evaluate red-tagged items

In this Section

The topics described in this section are located as indicated below:

Planning & Implementing 5S

Determine the Criteria for Red Tagging

Introduction

Certain types of unneeded items tend to accumulate in plants, offices and warehouses in predictable places. This section gives some pointers about the types of unneeded items that accumulate and where these items are often found.

Types of Unneeded Items

Some of the types of unneeded items that tend to accumulate are as follows:
- Defective or excess quantities of small parts or inventory
- Outdated or broken tools and inspection gear
- Old rags and other cleaning supplies
- Electrical equipment with broken cords
- Outdated posters, signs, and memos.

Places Where Unneeded Items Accumulate

Here are some of the locations where unneeded items tend to accumulate:
- In rooms or areas not designated for any particular purpose
- In corners next entrances or exits
- Along interior or exterior walls, next to partitions, and behind pillars
- Under the eaves of warehouses
- Under desks and shelves and in desk and cabinet drawers
- Near the bottom of tall stacks of items
- On unused management production schedule boards
- In tool boxes that are not clearly sorted.

Continued on next page

Determine the Criteria for Red Tagging, Continued

Figure 8: Typical
Red Tag Target

Planning & Implementing 5S

Applying Red Tags

Introduction	If done correctly, red tagging can produce impressive results. Keep in mind the following guidelines: • Set a number of Red Tags to be used • Apply one tag per item • Red-tag unneeded items • Red-tag excess needed items.
Set a Number of Red Tags To Be Used	Instead of handing them out as needed, determine in advance approximately how many red tags each workplace should use. Experience shows that you usually need an average of four tags per work area employee.
Apply One Tag per Item	When finding a shelf full of odds and ends, it is tempting to attach one red tag to the whole shelf. This will lead to confusion when items are to be disposed of, therefore individual tags should be attached to individual items. An exception might be where you have a lot of small items and they can be placed in a bag or box, sealed, and tagged.
Red-Tag Unneeded Items	Using a red-tag inspection sheet, walk through the target area and identify unneeded items or items that pose a safety hazard in their current location. If you are not certain about an item, red tag it! Perform red tagging as a team, and be sure to include team members who do not work in the target area regularly.

Continued on next page

Applying Red Tags, Continued

Red-Tag Excess Needed Items

We obviously want to red tag items that are unneeded. However, we should also red tag items that are needed if there are excessive amounts of them. Required amounts can be calculated based on the red-tagging criteria that have been set by the plant or your department. Everything in excess of these amounts should be removed from the target area.

Figure 9: Red Tag Inspection Check Sheet

Use the following check sheet as a guide:

Purpose	To ensure that you examine all potential items for red tagging
Directions	1. Examine all items under each category below for the entire target area 2. When you find an items that may not belong where it is, attach a red tag 3. When you have inspected an item under a category

Search these spaces		Search these storage places	
☐	Floors	☐	Shelves
☐	Aisles	☐	Racks
☐	Operation areas	☐	Closets
☐	Work stations	☐	Sheds
☐	Corners, behind / under equipment	☐	Other storage places
☐	Stairs	**Search the walls, boards, etc.**	
☐	Small rooms	☐	Items hung on walls
☐	Offices	☐	Bulleting boards
☐	Loading docks	☐	Sign boards
☐	Inside cabinets & drawers	☐	other

Continued on next page

Applying Red Tags, Continued

Figure 9: Red Tag Inspection Check Sheet (continued)

Look for unneeded equipment		Look for unneeded materials/supplies	
☐	Machines	☐	Raw materials
☐	Small tools	☐	Supplies
☐	Dies, jigs, bits	☐	Parts
☐	Conveyance equipment	☐	Work in progress
☐	Plumbing, pipes, etc.	☐	Finished products
☐	Electrical equipment	☐	Shipping materials
☐	Wire, fixtures, junction boxes	**Look for other unneeded items**	
Look for unneeded furniture		☐	Work clothes
☐	Cabinets	☐	Helmets
☐	Benches and tables	☐	Work shoes
☐	Chairs	☐	Trash cans
☐	Carts	☐	Other

Planning & Implementing 5S

Removing Red Tagged Items

Introduction	In order to implement the red-tag strategy effectively, a red tag holding are must be created. A red-tag holding area is an area set aside for use in storing red tagged items that need further evaluation. It gives you a safety net between first questioning whether something is needed, and actually getting rid of that item.
Red Tag Holding Areas	There are two types of red-tag holding areas required: • Central • Local.
Central Red-Tag Holding Area	The central red-tag holding area is used to manage the flow of items that cannot or should not be disposed of by individual departments or production areas.
Local Red-Tag Holding Area	Each department or production area that participates in red-tagging also needs a local red-tag holding area. The local red-tag holding area is used to manage the flow of items within a local department or production area.

Continued on next page

Planning & Implementing 5S

Removing Red Tagged Items, Continued

Evaluation of Red-tag Area

Once an item is red-tagged, it should be removed to the appropriate red-tag holding area. An evaluation team then inspects the red-tag holding area and determines the disposition of the red-tagged item.

Figure 10: Red Tag Holding Area

Planning & Implementing 5S

Disposition Red Tag Items

Introduction
Remove items that are not needed where they are and place them in a temporary red-tag holding area. This move frees the target area of clutter and temporarily stores the tagged items until their final disposition can be determined. <u>**Remember**</u> – **the decision to remove excess inventory may need to involve people other than those on your team**.

Evaluating Items
Remember that the Red-Tag Holding Area is for temporary storage only. Use the following list to help you decide where to relocate items or whether to recycle or otherwise dispose of them:

Category	Action
Obsolete	• Sell • Hold for depreciation • Give away • Throw away.
Defective	• Return to supplier • Throw away.
Scrap	• Remove from area to proper location.
Trash/garbage	• Throw away • Recycle.
Unneeded in this area	• Remove from area to proper location.
Used at least once a day	• Carry with you • Keep at place of use.
Used about once a week	• Store in area.
Used less than once a month	• Store where accessible in plant.
Seldom used	• Store in distant place • Sell • Give away • Throw away.
Use unknown	• Find out use • Remove from area to proper location.

Continued on next page

Planning & Implementing 5S

Disposition Red Tag Items, Continued

Figure 11: Items
in Red Tag
Holding Area

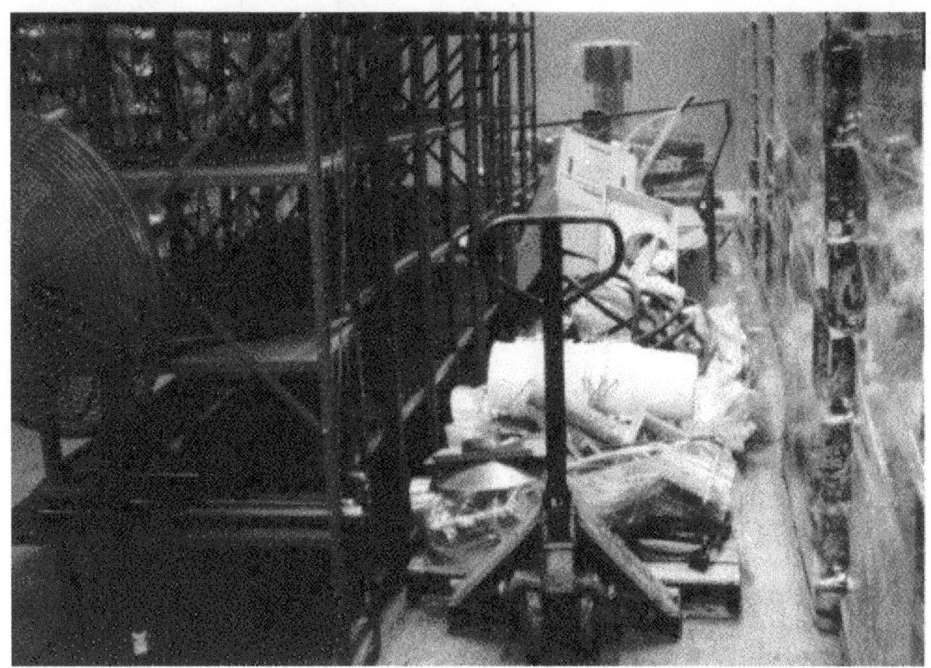

69

Planning & Implementing 5S

Set-In-Order

Overview

Introduction   This section describes the methodology for set in order.

Description   There are two steps to Set In Order:
- Decide appropriate locations
- Identify best locations.

Purpose   The purpose of the Set-In-Order phase is to eliminate the following kinds of waste:
- Motion waste
- Searching waste
- Waste of human energy
- Waste of excess inventory
- Waste of defective products
- Waste of unsafe conditions.

Procedure   Use the following procedure to implement Set-In-Order:

Step	Action
1	Decide upon appropriate locations for remaining items
2	Identify locations so that everyone will know: • what goes where, and • how many of each item belong in each location.

In this Section   The topics described in this section are located as indicated below

Topic	See Page
Analyze the Current Situation	72
Identify Target Issues	74
Decide Where to Keep Things	76
Make It Obvious Where Things Belong	77

Planning & Implementing 5S

Analyze the Current Situation

Introduction   Many types of waste and disorganization occur in the workplace. It is important to recognize them and eliminate them.

Analyze The Situation Procedure   Use the following procedure to analyze the current situation:

Step	Action
1	Review the VFA Problem Chart to look at the initial conditions observed by the team.
2	Review the VFA Feedback Chart. to see if anything has changed during the red-tagging.
3	Take additional photos if anything has changed significantly.
4	Review the workplace scan diagnostic checklist to see where your orderliness weaknesses remain.

Planning & Implementing 5S

Identify Target Issues

Introduction	The only way to effectively determine target issues to improve is by conducting an inspection of the target area and by using an observation checklist
Identifying Target Issues	Use the following procedure to identify target issues to improve for Set In Order:

Step	Action
1	Begin setting in order machines, large equipment, and workbenches.
2	Look at storage spaces such as shelves, racks, and inventory pallets.
3	Next, look at smaller equipment such as carts, chairs, and cans.
4	Consider small tools and supplies, including items kept in cabinets and drawers.
5	Look for areas where flow is restricted (i.e. where work in process is delayed; where people, materials, and machines get in each other's way; or where movement isn't smooth.

Continued on next page

Identify Target Issues, Continued

Figure 12:
Determining
Target issues

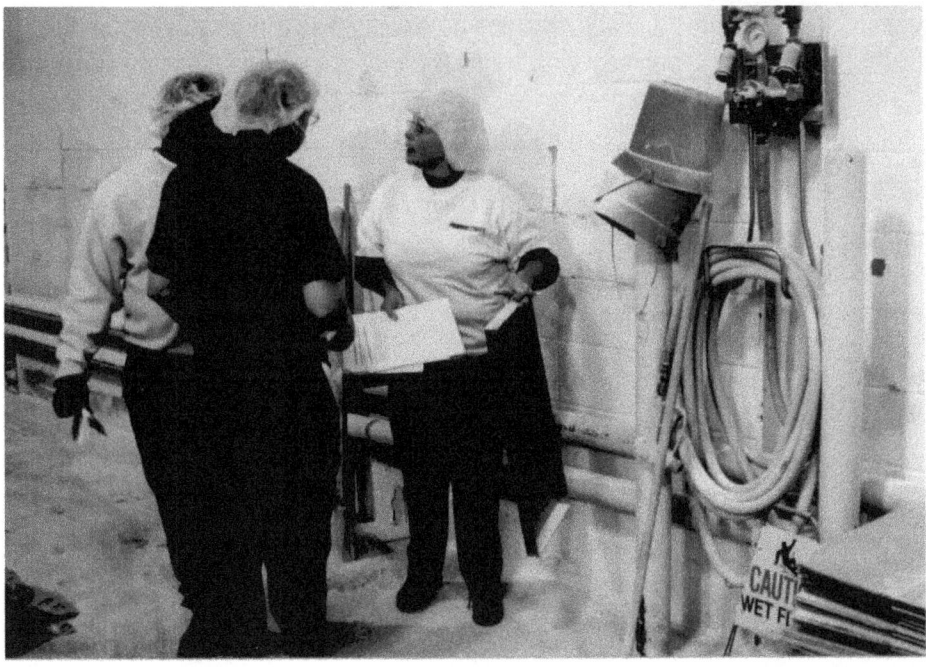

Decide Where to Keep Things

Introduction

It is crucial that everything be arranged so that anyone can understand where an item is kept, can easily and quickly pick it up and use it and can easily and quickly put it back in its proper place. This can only be accomplished if a place where everything belongs has been established.

Guidelines For Deciding Where Things Belong

Follow these guidelines for determining where things belong:
- The more often an item is used, the closer it should be to where it is used.
- Every items should have a designated name and location
- Make things easy to find and to put away properly
- Get things off of the floor whenever possible.

Other Considerations

In addition to the above guidelines, you should also consider the following:
- Store frequently used items near the place of use; store infrequently used items away from the place of use
- Store items together if they are used together and store them in the sequence that they are used
- Make storage places larger than the items stored so that they are physically easier to remove and put back.

Figure 13: Example Tool Arrangement

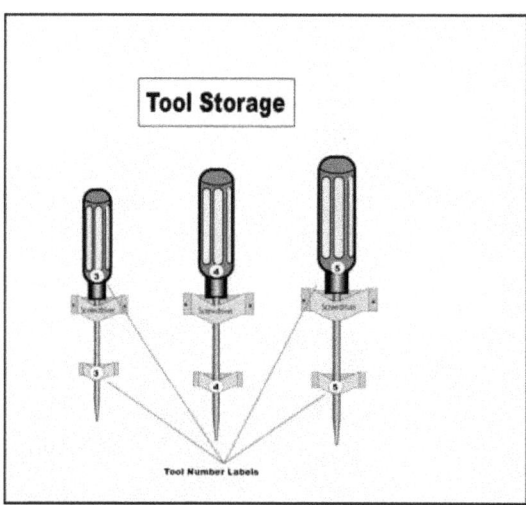

Planning & Implementing 5S

Make It Obvious Where Things Belong

Introduction

In plants and offices, everything should be easy to understand at a glance. The 5S program is designed to make the flow of goods, the identification of abnormalities, and various other aspects of plant or office operations visual enough so that anyone can quickly and easily understand what is happening.

Placement Strategies

Once it has been determined where things belong, the best place to put items must be decided so that everyone knows what goes where, and how many of each item belongs in each location. There are several different strategies for identifying what, where, and how much:

- Signboard Strategy
- Painting Strategy
- Color Coding Strategy
- Outlining Strategy.

Three Things To Remember

Three things to remember when employing the above strategies:

- Understand your audience, including the language they speak and where they are most likely to see, or read the visual indicator.
- Keep things simple! If something cannot be understood quickly, it is likely not to be followed.
- Use temporary materials to test your technique before you make it permanent.

In this section

The topics described in this unit are located as indicated below:

Topic	See Page
Signboard Strategy	78
Painting Strategy	79
Color Coding Strategy	83
Outlining Strategy	84

Planning & Implementing 5S

Signboard Strategy

Introduction

The Signboard Strategy uses signboards to identify what, where, and how many. The three main uses of signboards are:
- Location indicators, which show where items go
- Item indicators, which show what specific items go in those places
- Amount indicators, which show how many of these items belong there

Uses of Signboards

Signboards are often used to identify:
- Names of work areas
- Inventory locations
- Equipment storage locations
- Standard procedures
- Machine layout.

Signboard Strategy Procedure

Use the following procedure to implement the Signboard Strategy:

Step	Action
1	Determine locations • After consolidating remaining items, decide where to place them to best suit the way operations will be done • Be sure to put frequently used items as close as possible to the operators for easy retrieval.
2	Prepare locations • Organize shelving and cabinets in their specified places • Use your ingenuity.
3	Indicate locations • Make and post signboards that clearly indicate where each item belongs.

Continued on next page

78

Signboard Strategy, Continued

Signboard Strategy Procedure (continued)

Step	Action
4	Indicate item names • Make and post signboards that clearly indicate item names and the name/number of the shelf or cabinet where things belong.
5	Indicate Amounts • Indicate the number of inventory items covered by each signboard • Indicate both maximum and minimum amounts.
6	• Make orderliness a habit • Make orderliness a habit so that the workplace does not lapse back into disorder • Make Orderliness easy to maintain • Maintain discipline • Make 5S a daily habit.

Figure 14:
Example
Signboard
Layout

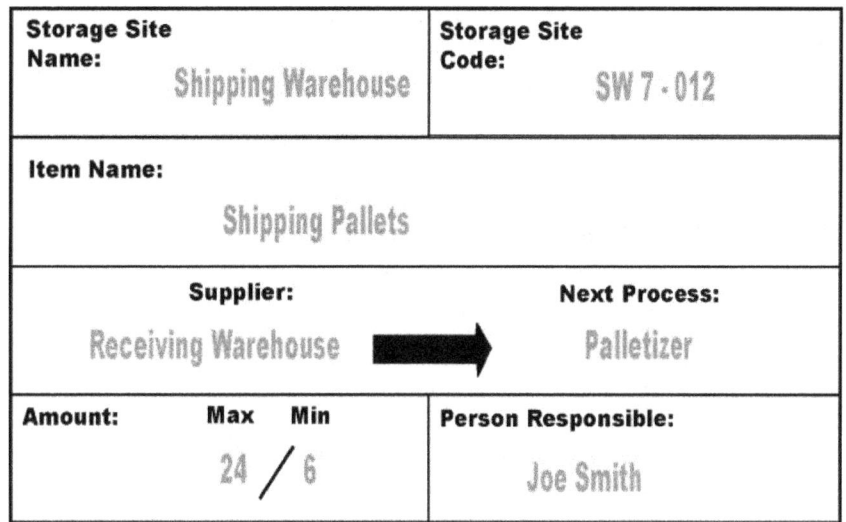

Planning & Implementing 5S

Painting Strategy

Introduction

The Painting Strategy is a method for identifying locations on floors and walkways. It is called the "Painting Strategy" because paint is the material generally used. However, acrylic sheets that can be cut into any length or width can also be used. Acrylics, although more expensive, shows up lust as clearly as paint, tends not to peel off as paint does, and is easy to clean.

Creating Divider Lines

The Painting Strategy is used to create divider lines that mark off the factory's walking areas ("walkways") from its working areas ("operation areas"). When mapping out walkways and operation areas, we should keep certain factors in mind:

- U-shaped cell designs are generally more efficient than straight production lines
- In-process inventory should be positioned carefully for best production flow
- Floors should be leveled or repaired if possible before divider lines are laid down
- Walkways should allow for safe and a smooth flow of goods by being wide enough and avoiding twists and turns
- Divider lines should be between 2 and 4 inches wide.
- Paint colors should be standardized, and the colors should be bright. An example of a color standard is:
  - Operation areas are green
  - Walkways are fluorescent orange
  - Divider lines are yellow.

Types of Divider Lines

Some types of divider lines include:

- Cart storage locations
- Aisle direction
- Door range, to show which war a door swings open
- Place markers for worktables
- Tiger marks, to show as where inventory and equipment should not be placed, or to show hazardous areas.

Continued on next page

Painting Strategy, Continued

Table 2 Divider Lines Used In Painting Strategy

The following are recommendations for different types of lines to be used in the plant:

Category	Sub Category	Color	Width	Comments
Floors	Operation area	Green		
	Walkway	Orange		Fluorescent Orange
	Rest area	Blue		
Lines	Area divider lines	Yellow	10 cm	Solid line
	Entrance & exit lines	Yellow	10 cm	Broken line
	Door-range lines	Yellow	10 cm	Broken line
	Direction lines	Yellow		Arrow
	Place markers (for in process inventory)	White	5 cm	Solid line
	Place markers (for operations)	White	5 cm	Corner lines
	Place markers (for defective goods	White	3 cm	Solid line

Continued on next page

Painting Strategy, Continued

Figure 15:
Applying Tiger
Stripe Lines

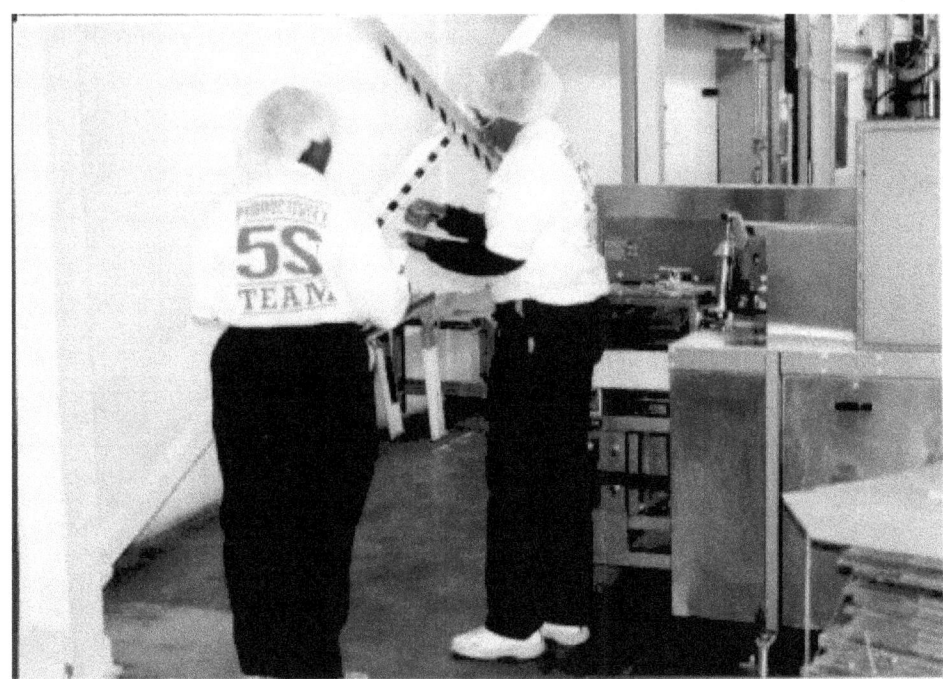

Planning & Implementing 5S

Color Coding Strategy

Introduction

Color-coding can be used to show clearly which materials or tools are used for which purpose. For example, if certain materials are to be used to make a particular product, they can all be color-coded with the same color and even stored in a location that is painted that color. Similarly, if different types of lubricants are to be used on different parts of a machine, the supply containers, oil cans, and machine parts can be color-coded to show what is used where.

Figure 16: Color Coded Containers

Planning & Implementing 5S

Outlining Strategy

Introduction

Outlining is a good way to show which tool is stored where. Outlining simply means drawing outlines of tools in their proper storage positions. When you want to return a tool, the outline provides an additional indication of where it belongs.

Figure 17: Example of Outlining

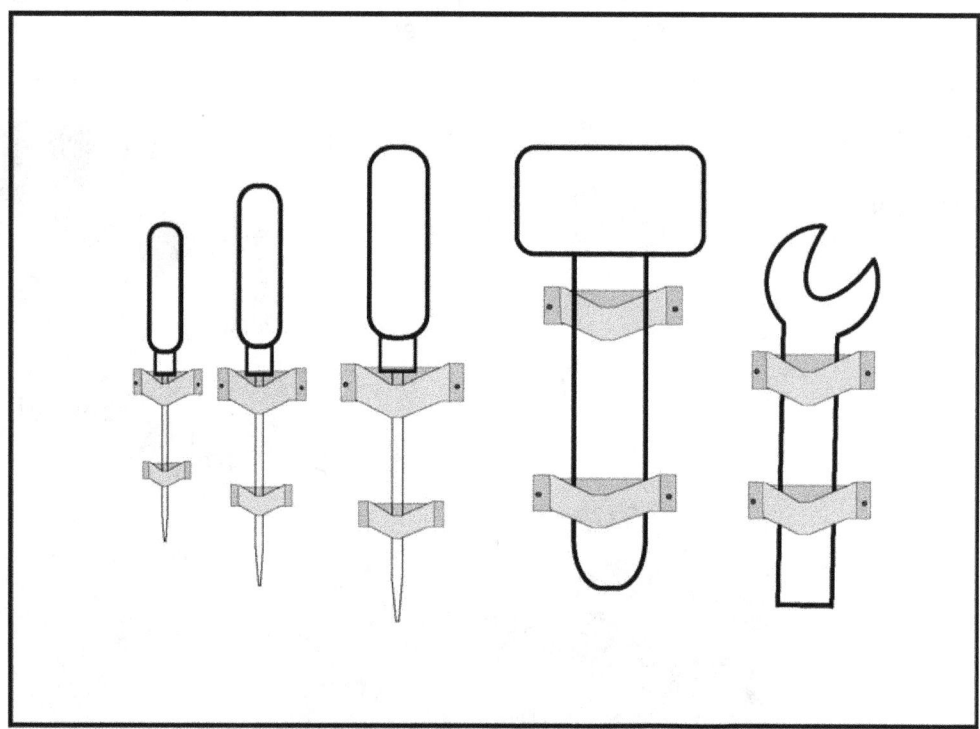

Shine

Overview

Introduction	This section describes the methodology for shine
Description	Daily cleanliness achieved through Shine activities are taught as a set of steps and rules that employees learn to maintain with discipline. The following steps should be taken to implement Shine: • Determine shine targets • Determine shine assignments • Determine shine methods • Prepare tools • Begin to shine.
Purpose	Cleaning may seem simple and obvious, and cleaning is probably already part of your routine in your workplace. In Shine, however, cleaning is not just to make things look good; it is a way to spot problems early and keep work areas and equipment in top operating condition at all times
Procedure	Use the following procedure to implement shine in your target area:

Step	Action
1	Identify shine targets.
2	Determine guidelines for cleaning.
3	Determine targets and assignments.
4	Perform Initial Cleaning.

In this Section The topics described in this section are located as indicated below

Topic	See Page
Determine Guidelines for Cleaning	86
Determine Targets and Assignments	89
Determine Cleaning Methods	89
Creating Standards for Shine Procedures	93
Replace Worn Hoses, Wires, and Tubing	93

Planning & Implementing 5S

Determine Guidelines for Cleaning

Introduction

Sweeping and wiping are the two fundamental activities in cleanliness. The guidelines for your work area must be built on this foundation.

Table 3 Cleanliness Phases

Use the following table to help you determine the cleaning guidelines for your work area:

Phase	Step	Description
1	Daily Cleanliness – Making things clean	Make cleanliness a part of daily duties (e.g., sweep and wipe away dirt, grime, and dust daily) • Sweep, mop, and wipe floors, walkways, and shelves until they shine. • Scrub away grit and debris that has become caked onto oily equipment surfaces until the equipment shines.
2	Cleanliness Inspections – Using your senses	Once cleanliness takes root as a daily practice, maintain conditions by using your senses to detect slight defects or other abnormalities • Pay close attention not only to the main section of each machine, but also its moving parts and drive chain. • Check for proper amounts of oil, air, and ventilation.

Continued on next page

Planning & Implementing 5S

Determine Guidelines for Cleaning, Continued

Table 3 Cleanliness Phases (continued)

Phase	Step	Description
3	Cleanliness Maintenance – Making improvements	Once a defect is discovered, make certain that it is repaired. • If the operator can quickly fix or improve the slight defect, this should be considered part of the operator's "Cleanliness Inspection" duties • If not a maintenance request should be completed and turned in.

**Figure 18:
Typical Product
Debris**

Planning & Implementing 5S

Determine Targets and Assignments

Introduction

Workplace cleanliness is the responsibility of everyone who works there. The first step is to divide the workspace into specific cleanliness areas or targets and then assign these areas to individuals to clean and maintain.

Categories Of Cleanliness Targets

Cleanliness targets consist of three categories:
- Warehouse items
- Equipment
- Space.

Categories Details

The following are examples of the three categories:

Target	Description
Warehouse items	Raw materials, procured parts, minor ingredients, ingredients, finished products, semi-finished products, hold items.
Equipment	Machines, tools, inspection instruments, conveyance tools, work tables, cabinets, desks, chairs, and spare equipment.
Space	Floors, work areas, walkways, walls, pillars, ceilings, windows, shelves, closets, rooms, and lights.

Continued on next page

Planning & Implementing 5S

Determine Targets and Assignments, Continued

Assignment Procedure

Use the following procedure when determining targets and assignments:

Step	Action
1	Draw a map of the workplace target area
2	Review the Categories on the previous page and decide which areas should be designated as cleanliness targets.
3	Mark the cleanliness target areas on the map
4	Mark the name of the person responsible for each target area on the map (on each target area identified).

Figure 19: Workplace Map With Cleanliness Targets

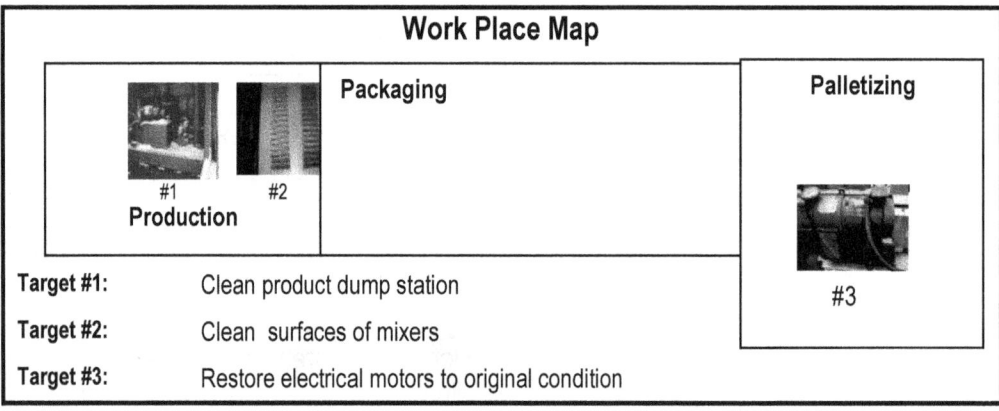

Work Place Map

Production
#1 #2

Packaging

Palletizing
#3

Target #1:   Clean product dump station

Target #2:   Clean surfaces of mixers

Target #3:   Restore electrical motors to original condition

Planning & Implementing 5S

Determine Cleaning Methods

Introduction	Daily cleanliness activities should include not only what is required at the end of the work shift but also "cleanliness inspections" before the shift starts. These activities are the foundation of Cleanliness.
Telling People What To Do	Unless people know exactly what to do, they are likely to spend most of the allotted time just getting ready to clean. To use the time efficiently, people need specific procedures to follow. A DPS and a cleanliness checklist should be developed for each cleanliness activity.
In this section	The topics described in this section are located as indicated below:

Topic	See Page
Determine tools required	92
Creating standards for Shine procedures	93
Developing a cleaning/inspection checklist	95

Planning & Implementing 5S

Determine Tools Required

Introduction

After all of the targets have been determined and assignments made, the tools necessary for carrying out the cleaning must be determined. The tools required for each task will be spelled out in each DPS and Checklist.

Tool Considerations

Consider the following when determining the tools needed:
- Cleanliness starts with a thorough sweeping using brooms – especially on production floors and the maintenance shop where debris accumulates on the floor.
- A mop is similar to a broom but functions as a rag for wiping floors.
- Rags are the main tools for cleaning worktables, office desks, and equipment surfaces. Use damp rags on surfaces that collect dust or grime. Dry rags are better for polishing and wiping oily areas.

Figure 20: Cleaning Tools

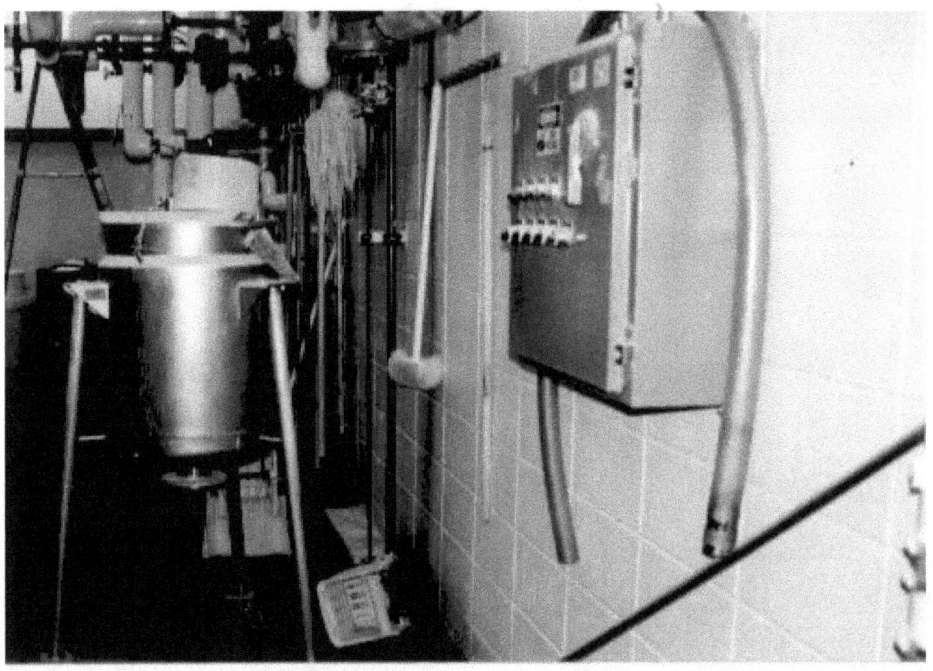

Planning & Implementing 5S

Creating Standards for Shine Procedures

Introduction

It is not enough for people to know what to do, it is important for them to know well each task must be done. Standards will provide the scale against which each task may be measured.

Criteria

Use the following criteria for determining standards for Shine procedures:

Step	Action
	Inventory Items
1	All dust removed from products, parts, or materials.
2	All dirt removed from inventory storage shelve.
3	All dirt removed from in-process inventory storage sites.
4	All dirt removed from pallets used to move inventory items.
	Equipment
5	All dust and oil removed from the vicinity of equipment.
6	All water, oil and debris removed from underneath equipment.
7	All dirt, dust and oil removed from surfaces of equipment.
8	All dirt removed from glass displays such as gauges or oil indicators.
9	All equipment covers and lids removed in order to wipe a way inside dirt.
10	All dirt, dust and oil removed from pneumatic pipes and electrical cables.
11	All dirt, dust and oil removed from limit switches and other switches.
12	All dirt, dust and oil removed from light bulbs and tubes.
13	All dirt and dust removed from inspection instruments.

Continued on next page

93

Planning & Implementing 5S

Creating Standards for Shine Procedures, Continued

Criteria (continued)

Step	Action
	Spaces
14	All dirt, dust and trash removed from floor spaces and walkways .
15	All water and oil puddles removed from floor spaces and walkways .
16	All dirt and dust removed from walls windows, and ledges.
17	All dirt and dust removed from ceilings and beams.
18	All dust removed from light fixtures.
19	All dirt and dust removed from shelves and work tables.
20	All trash and empty containers removed from the vicinity of the building.
21	The building's exterior walls washed.

Figure 21: 5 Minute Shine

Planning & Implementing 5S

Developing a Cleaning/Inspection Checklist

Introduction

The Cleaning/Inspection Checklist is used to ensure that all potential surfaces and areas that require inspection and cleaning are covered.

Cleaning Considerations

In addition to the standards, consider the following suggestions when developing the Cleaning/Inspection Checklist:

- Sweep away dirt from floor cracks, wall corners, and around posts and pillars
- Wipe of dirt and dust from walls, windows and doors
- Be thorough about cleaning dirt, dust, debris, product scraps, oil, and other foreign matter from all surfaces. Try to restore to the surface's original state
- Use approved cleaning or polishing agents when simple sweeping or wiping is not enough to remove dirt or stains
- Cleanliness is an activity that everyone should take part in – especially people who work with the machines or in target areas.

Continued on next page

Developing a Cleaning/Inspection Checklist, Continued

**Table 4
Inspection Points
Related To
Target
Phenomena**

Use the following table to determine inspection procedures and checklist items:

No	Phenomena	Point	Main Response
1	Dirt and Grime	Dust, grime, dirt, debris, product scrap, etc	Cleaning
2	Oil	Oil leakage, oil stains, oil depletion, incorrect oil type, oil clogging	Add oil, change oil, clean and repair
3	Temperature and Pressure	Over heating, insufficient heating, excess pressure, insufficient pressure, abnormal coolant temperature, off-standard control devices	Repair to restore original states
4	Looseness and slack	Loose or missing bolts, loose or missing nuts, slack belts, broken welds	Tighten, replace or repair to restore original state
5	Damage	Broken or cracked hoses, broken meters, cracked glass, damaged switches, broken wires, damaged mechanical arms, vibration in rotary mechanisms	Replace and repair to restore original state

Continued on next page

Planning & Implementing 5S

Developing a Cleaning/Inspection Checklist, Continued

Procedure for Developing a Checklist

Use the following procedure to develop a Cleaning/Inspection Checklist:

Step	Action
1	In the first column under "Mechanism", describe the mechanisms to be covered. Include a picture or flow diagram if necessary.
2	In the second column, place the step number
3	Under the "Point Column, place the inspection point, in the form of a question.
4	Place an "X" under the appropriate heading under the "Main Response" column. Use Table 4 to determine response.

Continued on next page

Planning & Implementing 5S

Developing a Cleaning/Inspection Checklist, Continued

Figure 22: Example of a Checklist

The following figure is an example of what an inspection checklist should look like.

Mechanism	No	Inspection Point	Main Response			
			Clean	Lubricate	Replace	Repair
Cartoner	1	Is there any dirt grime or debris present?	X			
	2	Do oil level indicators show adequate levels?		X		
	3	Are safety devices functioning properly?			X	X
	4	Is there a build up of glue on interior surfaces?	X			
	5	Are plows and guides in proper place and securely attached?			X	X
	6	Do cartons move through the mechanism with out jamming?	X			X

(Callout boxes on the left labeled 1, 2, 3, 4 point to Mechanism column, No column, Inspection Point column, and Main Response header respectively.)

Planning & Implementing 5S

Standardize

Overview

Introduction
This section describes the methodology for standardize.

Description
Standardize differs from Sort, Set In Order, and Shine, all of which are activities. In contrast, Standardize is the result of continuous maintenance of the first three activities (sometimes known as 3S). Standardize means finding ways to make the 3S activities into a habit.

Purpose
Standardize prevents, the following problems from arising:
- Conditions go back to their undesirable levels
- At the end of the shift, piles of unneeded items are left from the day's work activities and lie around the production equipment.
- Tool storage sites become disorganized and must be put back in order at the end of each shift
- Production debris fall on the floor and must be swept up.

Procedure
Use the following procedure to standardize 5S:

Step	Action
1	Establish guidelines for (3S) conditions of: • Sort • Set In Order • Shine
2	Attain those conditions.
3	Write the standards into a Standard Operating Procedure
4	Make the standard visual.
5	Maintain and monitor these conditions.

In this Section
The topics described in this section are located as indicated below

Topic	See Page
Establish Guidelines for 3S Conditions	101
Write Standard Operating Procedure	105
Make Standard Guidelines Visible	111
Maintain and Monitor 3S Conditions	112

Planning & Implementing 5S

Establish Guidelines for 3S Conditions

Introduction

3S activities are the first three steps of the 5S program:
- Sort
- Set In Order
- Shine.

Purpose

The purpose for establishing 3S guidelines is to identify and communicate the conditions you want to maintain for each of these activities.

In this section

The topics described in this section are located as indicated below:

Topic	See Page
Determining 3 S responsibilities	103
Determining 3S Methods	104

Planning & Implementing 5S

Determining 3 S Responsibilities

Introduction

When it comes to maintaining 3S conditions, unless everyone knows exactly what they are responsible for doing and when, where, and how to do it, neither Sort, Set In Order, or Shine has any meaning. It is essential that people be given clear job assignments based on their own workplaces.

5S Maps

The 5S map is a useful tool for assigning responsibilities. 5S maps show how the workplace is divided into sections and list the names of the people responsible for maintaining 5S conditions in those areas. This makes 5S job assignments visible at a glance.

Figure 23: 5S Map With Improvement Tags Attached

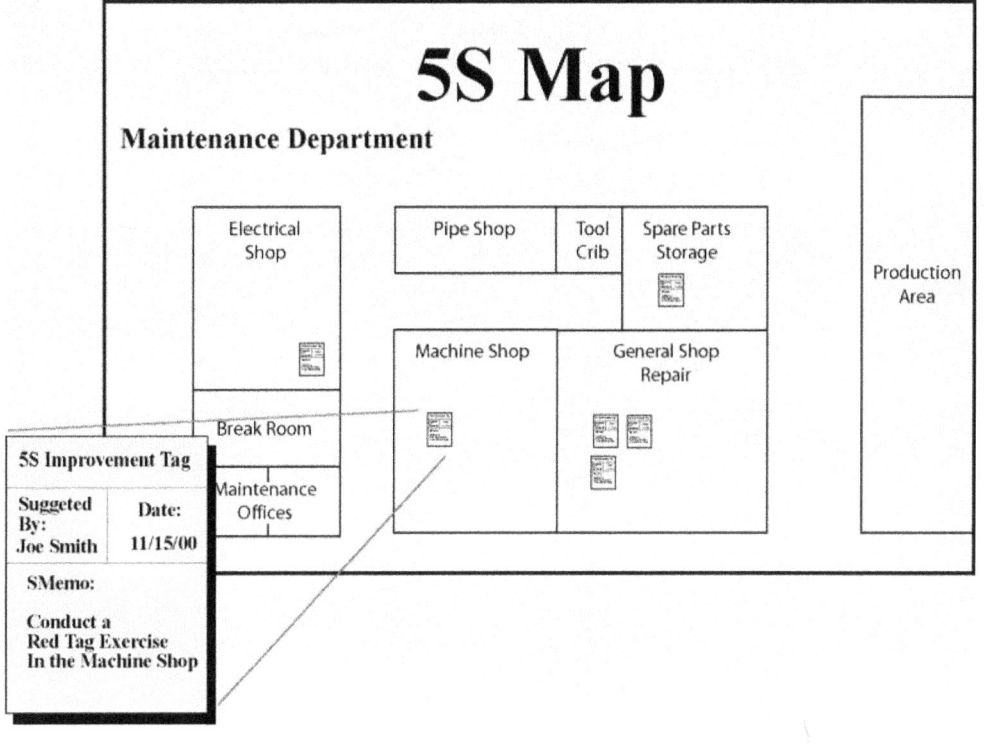

Determining 3S Methods

Introduction

The correct methodology for Sort, Set In Order, and Shine must be identified and planned for in advance. The planning team must process map what is required for each of these 3S steps.

Process Mapping Methods

Process mapping involves each of the following actions:

- Diagram (map) the way work is currently done, using a flow chart to graphically portray the process. Members who come up with ideas for improvements should write them down and wait for the next steps.
- Identify problem areas to concentrate on (circling the areas in red may help).
- Create possible action steps — but postpone judgment; the emphasis should be on generating ideas and writing them down on charts all can see.
- Evaluate action steps and select those which are fastest and easiest to implement, and have the most significant effects. The others should be held for future meetings.
- Make one team member responsible for each action step.
- Set firm follow-up and completion dates, including a date for the next meeting.

Identifying Required Tools and Materials

Once you have process mapped the target area for each of the 3S steps, identify all of the tools, equipment, and materials required to complete each process. Transfer this information to an SOP Information page once you have agreement of the team.

Planning & Implementing 5S

Write Standard Operating Procedures

Introduction

A Standard Operating Procedure (SOP) is a set of written instructions that document a routine or repetitive 3S activity followed by an organization. The development and use of SOPs are an integral part of a successful 5S system as it provides individuals with the information to perform a job properly, and facilitates consistency in the quality and integrity of a process.

Purpose

SOPs detail the regularly recurring 3S processes that are to be conducted or followed within an organization. They document the way activities are to be performed to facilitate consistent conformance to process and quality system requirements and to support data quality. They may describe, for example, fundamental programmatic actions such as shine procedures, technical actions such as audit processes, and processes for maintaining, and using equipment. SOPs are intended to be specific to the organization or facility whose activities are described and assist that organization to sustain their 3S processes as well as ensure compliance with governmental regulations. If not written correctly, SOPs are of limited value. In addition, the best written SOPs will fail if they are not followed. Therefore, the use of SOPs needs to be reviewed and re-enforced by management, preferably the direct supervisor. Current copies of the SOPs also need to be readily accessible for reference in the work areas of those individuals actually performing the activity, either in hardcopy or electronic format, otherwise SOPs serve little purpose.

Writing Styles

SOPs should be written in a concise, step-by-step, easy-to-read format. The information presented should be unambiguous and not overly complicated. The active voice and present verb tense should be used. The term "you" should not be used, but implied. The document should not be wordy, redundant, or overly lengthy. Keep it simple and short. Information should be conveyed clearly and explicitly to remove any doubt as to what is required. Also, use a flow chart to illustrate the process being described. In addition, follow the style guide used by your organization, e.g., font size and margins.

Continued on next page

Planning & Implementing 5S

Write Standard Operating Procedures, Continued

SOP Preparation

The 5S Planning team should have a procedure in place for determining what procedures or processes need to be documented. Those SOPs should then be written by individuals knowledgeable with the activity and the organization's internal structure. These individuals are essentially subject-matter experts who actually perform the work or use the process. A team approach can be followed, especially for multi-tasked processes where the experiences of a number of individuals are critical, which also promotes "buy-in" from potential users of the SOP.

SOPs should be written with sufficient detail so that someone with limited experience with or knowledge of the procedure, but with a basic understanding, can successfully reproduce the procedure when unsupervised. The experience requirement for performing an activity should be noted in the section on personnel qualifications.

SOP Review and Approval

SOPs should be reviewed (that is, validated) by one or more individuals with appropriate training and experience with the process. It is especially helpful if draft SOPs are actually tested by individuals other than the original writer before the SOPs are finalized. The finalized SOPs should be approved as described in the organization's 5S Implementation Plan or its own SOP for preparation of SOPs. Generally the immediate supervisor reviews and approves each SOP. Signature approval indicates that an SOP has been both reviewed and approved by management.

Frequency of Revisions and Reviews

SOPs need to remain current to be useful. Therefore, whenever procedures are changed, SOPs should be updated and re-approved. If desired, modify only the pertinent section of an SOP and indicate the change date/revision number for that section in the Table of Contents and the document control notation. SOPs should be also systematically reviewed on a periodic basis, e.g. every 1-2 years, to ensure that the policies and procedures remain current and appropriate, or to determine whether the SOPs are even needed. The review date should be added to each SOP that has been reviewed. If an SOP describes a process that is no longer followed, it should be withdrawn from the current file and archived.

The review process should not be overly cumbersome to encourage timely review. The frequency of review should be indicated by management in the organization's 5S Implementation Plan. That plan should also indicate the individual(s) responsible for ensuring that SOPs are current.

Continued on next page

Write Standard Operating Procedures, Continued

Checklists

Many activities use checklists to ensure that steps are followed in order. Checklists are also used to document completed actions. Any check lists or forms included as part of an activity should be referenced at the points in the procedure where they are to be used and then attached to the SOP.

In some cases, detailed checklists are prepared specifically for a given activity. In those cases, the SOP should describe, at least generally, how the checklist is to be prepared, or on what it is to be based. Copies of specific checklists should be then maintained in the file with the activity results and/or with the SOP.

Remember that the checklist is not the SOP, but a part of the SOP

Document Control

Each organization should develop a numbering system to systematically identify and label their SOPs, and the document control should be described in its overall Quality Management Plan and reflected in the 5S Implementation plan. Generally, each page of an SOP should have control documentation notation, similar to that illustrated in Figure 24. A short title and identification (ID) number can serve as a reference designation. The revision number and date are very useful in identifying the SOP in use when reviewing historical data and is critical when the need for evidentiary records is involved and when the activity is being reviewed. When the number of pages is indicated, the user can quickly check if the SOP is complete. Generally this type of document control notation is located in the upper right-hand corner of each document page following the title page.

Figure 24: SOP Document Control Notation

Short Title/ID #
Rev. #:
Date:
Page 1 of

Continued on next page

Write Standard Operating Procedures, Continued

SOP General Format

SOPs should be organized to ensure ease and efficiency in use and to be specific to the organization which develops it. There is no one "correct" format; and internal formatting will vary with each organization and with the type of SOP being written. Where possible break the information into a series of logical steps to avoid a long list. The level of detail provided in the SOP may differ based on, e.g., whether the process is critical, the frequency of that procedure being followed, the number of people who will use the SOP, and where training is not routinely available.

Generally the SOP will contain the following sections:
- Title Page
- Table of Context

Title Page

The first page or cover page of each SOP should contain the following information: a title that clearly identifies the activity or procedure, an SOP identification (ID)number, date of issue and/or revision, the name of the applicable agency, division, and/or branch to which this SOP applies, and the signatures and signature dates of those individuals who prepared and approved the SOP. An example is shown in Figure 25.

Figure 25: 5S SOP Title Page

Cleaning and Inspection of Line 7 Equipment

5S Standard Operating Procedure

13 021

By

Bill Jones

APPROVED

Supervisor Line 7 & 8   4/16/2013 Date

Plant Manager   4/16/2013 Date

Table of Contents

A Table of Contents may be needed for quick reference, especially if the SOP is long, for locating information and to denote changes or revisions made only to certain sections of an SOP.

Continued on next page

Write Standard Operating Procedures, Continued

Supporting Information Page

Well-written SOPs should first briefly describe the purpose of the work or process, including any regulatory information or standards that are appropriate to the SOP process, and the scope to indicate what is covered. Define any specialized or unusual terms either in a separate definition section or in the appropriate discussion section. Denote what sequential procedures should be followed, divided into significant sections; e.g., possible interferences, equipment needed, personnel qualifications, and safety considerations (preferably listed in bold to capture the attention of the user).

Figure 26: Supporting Information Page

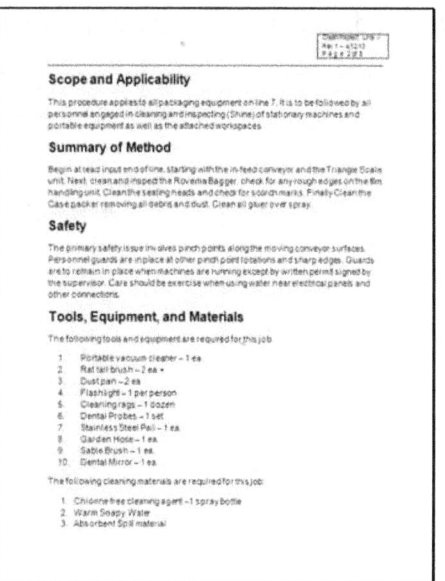

Continued on next page

Write Standard Operating Procedures, Continued

Writing Procedure Steps

All information should be grouped into small, manageable units. The information grouped in a unit should relate to one relevant point based on its purpose or function. Information presented should use consistent words, labels, formats, organizations, and sequences. Figure 27 uses a step action table to incorporate the above procedure writing principles, The steps are organized under subheadings such as "Pre-Cleaning, Cleaning, and Inspection" as shown in below. This style of writing is known as Information Mapping.

People can typically remember about 7 – 9 steps, therefore you should not have more than 9 steps without organizing the steps under a common heading and if more stpes are required, create additional chunks of procedure steps.

Figure 27: Procedure Pages

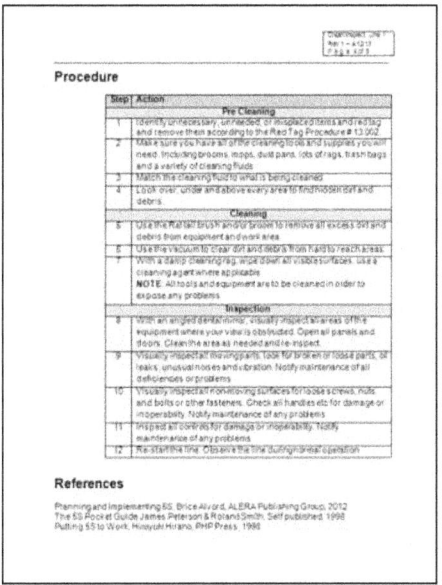

More on Information Mapping

If you want to learn more, I suggest one or more of the following:

- Attend an Information Mapping course. The Information Mapping company provides training programs on the method, and it comes from the owners of the method.

- Read a description of the seven principles at TechWriter Wiki.

Planning & Implementing 5S

Make Standard Guidelines Visible

Introduction

In this unit you will make the temporary visual techniques you implemented in Set-In-Order. You will:
- Make temporary lines permanent by painting
- Replace temporary lines and signboards with permanent ones
- Use color-coding to aid visual orderliness.

Figure 28: Making Lines Permanent

Purpose

Because people control and manage the work area, it is essential that everyone be able to tell the difference between what is correct and what is incorrect.

Why Visual Techniques

Visual techniques such as lines, labels and signboards make it possible to grasp the standard at a glance and immediately correct any variance.

111

Maintain and Monitor 3S Conditions

Introduction — This unit explains why it is important to maintain and monitor 3S conditions

Purpose — Optimum 5S conditions are not likely to be maintained unless everyone knows:
- Exactly what he or she is responsible for doing
- When to do it
- Where it is to be done
- How to do it.

Effective Tool — The 5S Area Map is the most effective tool for displaying 5S responsibilities and procedures.

Figure 29: The 5S Area Map

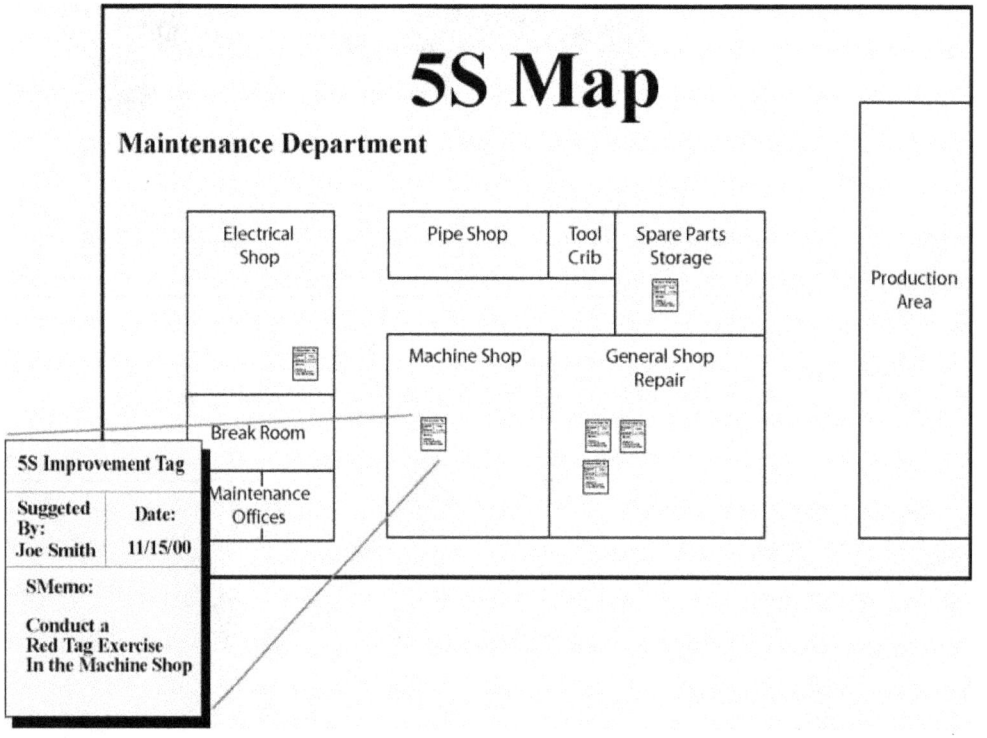

Planning & Implementing 5S

Sustain

Overview

Introduction

This section describes the methodology for sustain.

Description

The implementation of Sustain is different from that of the first four pillars in the sense that the results are not visible and cannot be measured. Commitment to it exists in people's hearts and minds and only their behavior shows its presence. Because of this, it cannot be implemented like a technique. However, you can create conditions that encourage the implementation of the Sustain pillar.

Purpose

People usually commit themselves to sustaining a particular course of action because the rewards for keeping to the course of action are greater than the rewards for departing from it. Without your commitment to sustain the 5S activities, implementation of the first four pillars falls apart.

Procedure

Use the following procedure to plan methods to sustain the 5S standards and guidelines:

Step	Action
1	Identify the standards, guidelines and record them on a Sustain Planning Worksheet.
2	Identify the people or groups of people from whom adherence to the 5S standards, guidelines, and procedures is necessary.
3	Determine the methods you will use to get adherence to the standards and guidelines and when each method should take place.
4	Use a 5S Sustaining Plan Sheet to create your plan.

In this Section

The topics described in this section are located as indicated below

Topic	See Page
Create a Plan for Sustain	114
Train People in the Target Area	117
Create and Maintain a 5S Communications Board	124
Make 5s Part of Daily Work	125
Auditing 3S activities	126

Planning & Implementing 5S

Create a Plan for Sustain

Introduction

There are five conditions required to make a habit of the beneficial changes you have made in the target area:

- Development of new Awareness and skills
- Support from management
- Ongoing company wide communication
- Making 5S standards part of daily work
- Total employee involvement.

Your plan needs to incorporate all five of these elements.

Development Of New Awareness And Skills

Training is an essential tool for building a shared understanding of the 5S system and developing the skills to support the 5S standards. The following are ways to provide this training to others:

- Use the video tape series from this class to show others
- Photograph or video tape your own examples to show others the value of 5S
- A one-point lesson can be used to give a concise, visual explanation of how to perform a 5S task
- A DPS sheet can be used to show the procedure for performing a 5S task.

Support From Management

Managers can give a great deal of support for 5S implementation by providing rewards, recognition, and resources. Management support and involvement is critical. The program cannot succeed without it!

Ongoing Company Wide Communication

There are many ways to spread the word about 5S, including the following:

- A 5S communication board
- Meetings
- 5S newsletter.

Continued on next page

Planning & Implementing 5S

Create a Plan for Sustain, Continued

Making 5S Standards Part Of Daily Work

Sustaining 5S standards means making them part of everyone's daily work. This means that they are considered part of the job, not something extra. Two methods that can help are:
- Five-minute 5S – at the end of the shift, everyone takes 5 or 10 minutes to sort, set in order, and shine their own work area
- Weekly 5S – once a week everyone in the area sets aside approximately 30 minutes to perform the activities together.

Total Employee Involvement

Employees can learn a lot from working with each other. When everyone is involved in 5S activities, the system can take root in a lasting way.

Figure 30: Performing 5 Minute 5S

Planning & Implementing 5S

Train People in the Target Area

Introduction

As mentioned earlier, a one-point lesson can be used to give a concise, visual explanation of how to perform a 5S task. A one-point lesson is a 5 to 10 minute self-study lesson drawn up by team members and covering a single aspect of equipment or machine structure, functioning, or method of inspection.

Purpose of a One-Point Lesson

One-point lessons have three purposes:
- To help sharpen equipment-related knowledge and skills and communicate information about specific problems and improvements
- To share important information easily when it is needed
- To improve the performance of the entire team.

The Basic Philosophy of One-Point Lessons

The basic philosophy behind the one point lesson is simple:
- Develop and research the lessons yourselves
- Make up your own lesson sheets
- Explain them to all team members
- Discuss them openly on the production floor
- Improve them.

Continued on next page

Planning & Implementing 5S

Train People in the Target Area, Continued

Types of One-Point Lessons

Depending on their purpose, one-point lesson sheets fall into one of three categories:
- Basic knowledge lessons
- Examples of problems
- Examples of improvements.

Basic Knowledge Lessons

These are training tools designed to fill in knowledge gaps and ensure that team members have the knowledge they need for daily production and QCD activities. These lessons may focus on equipment subsystems, safety points, quality, GMPs, or basic operating information.

Examples of Problems

Based on problems that have actually occurred; these lessons are designed to communicate knowledge or skills to help operators prevent similar problems from happening in the future.

Examples Of Improvements

To ensure that successful improvement ideas are used widely, these lessons present what needs to be done to prevent or correct equipment abnormalities by describing the approaches, actions, and results of specific improvement projects.

Continued on next page

Planning & Implementing 5S

Train People in the Target Area, Continued

Presenting the One-Point Lesson

Here is how to present a one-point lesson:
1. Present the theme and explain the motivating reason for writing the lesson
2. As you go through the lesson, ask questions of the group; try to get them to examine their own knowledge and behavior relating to the theme
3. Don't rely on only the lesson sheet. Demonstrate the lesson using actual objects or parts involved whenever possible
4. ask people questions after the presentation and follow up to make sure that everyone has understood
5. Repeat the lesson several times if necessary, until you are sure that it has been linked to action.

Figure 31: Presenting the One-Point Lesson

Planning & Implementing 5S

Developing One-Point Lessons

Introduction

A One-point lesson is primarily a means of communication best practices about processes and equipment. It is crucial that you put some time and thought into the development of a one-point lesson. Remember, a workplace where information is shared is the most productive kind of work environment.

Tips for Writing One-Point Lessons

To make sure that everyone has a common understanding of the lessons, keep in mind the following points when making up the lessons:

- Choose a theme based on a common problem the workplace is currently facing
- Don't just describe the problem with words, use drawings, photographs, or cartoons so everyone can grasp what is important
- Adapt the form to your particular needs
- For examples of problems, make up the lessons immediately after the problem has occurred and then teach it while the issue is fresh in everyone's mind.

Continued on next page

Developing One-Point Lessons, Continued

Procedure for Writing One-Point Lessons

Use the following procedure to develop a one-point lesson:

Step	Action
1	Determine the nature of the lesson you are going to develop:

If...	Then...
Basic knowledge	Discuss the topic with other team members to get their input or ideas. See if there is already a one-point lesson on the topic.
Problem	Discuss the topic with other team members to get their input or ideas. Then discuss it with your supervisor. Get permission to proceed with a one-point lesson.
Improvement	Discuss the topic with other team members to get their input or ideas. Make a suggestion in your Green Room Meeting and wait until it is approved.

Step	Action
2	Mark the appropriate box at the top of the form
3	Determine a theme for your lesson and write it in the space provided.

Continued on next page

Developing One-Point Lessons, Continued

Procedure for Writing One-Point Lessons (continued)

Step	Action
	Writing The Lesson
4	On a separate piece of paper, make an outline of what you want to present. Remember to review the tips on page .
5	Add additional information to explain the lines in the outline. Keep it simple and to the point. Follow the example in Figure 29.
	Writing The Lesson (continued)
6	Transfer the information to the one-point lesson form.
7	Add a diagram or picture to illustrate your point.
8	Add call out boxes to highlight the steps in your lesson. See Figure 32.
	Getting Approval
9	Review your lesson with a team member to get their input and ideas. Make any needed corrections.
10	Submit the form to your supervisor for approval.

Continued on next page

Developing One-Point Lessons, Continued

**Figure 32:
Example of A
One-Point
Lesson**

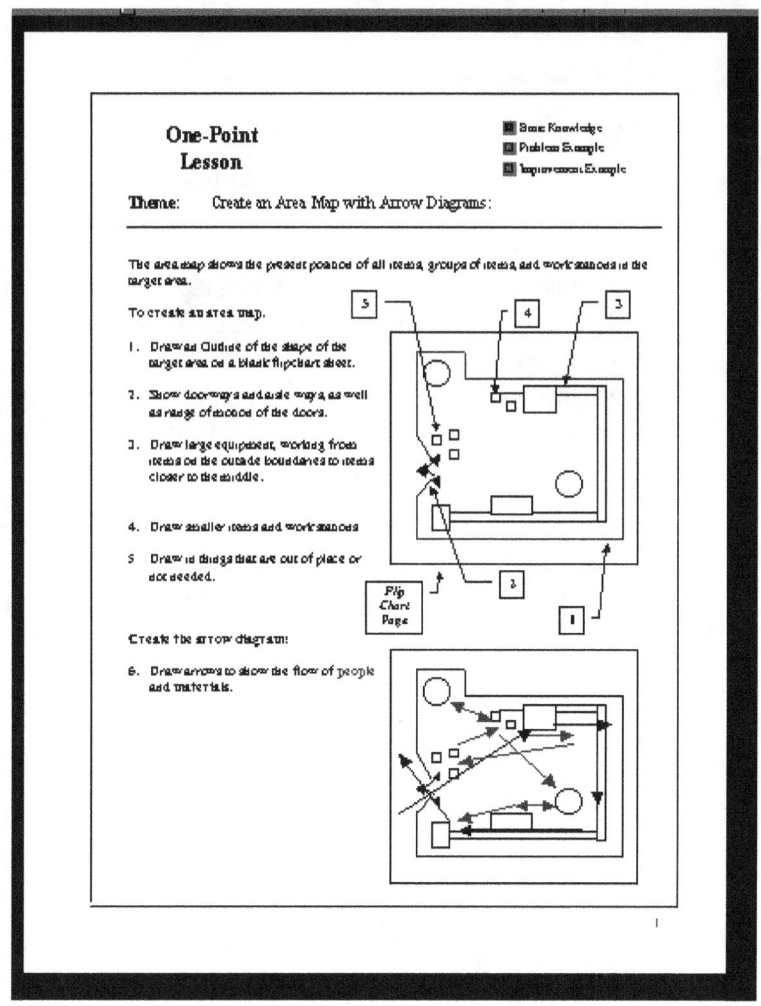

Planning & Implementing 5S

Create and Maintain a 5S Communications Board

Introduction

This unit describes the 5S map.

Purpose

5S Maps define territories of the people responsible for maintaining 5S conditions and allow for communication and submission of improvement ideas.

Improvement Tags

An effective map features improvement tags such as the one shown in Figure 33.These tags which can be as simple as a memo pad or complex as a specially designed tag, allow people to attach ideas to the appropriate place on the map. This allows anyone passing through the area who notices something in the workplace that needs improvement to communicate their ideas.

Figure 33: 5S Map

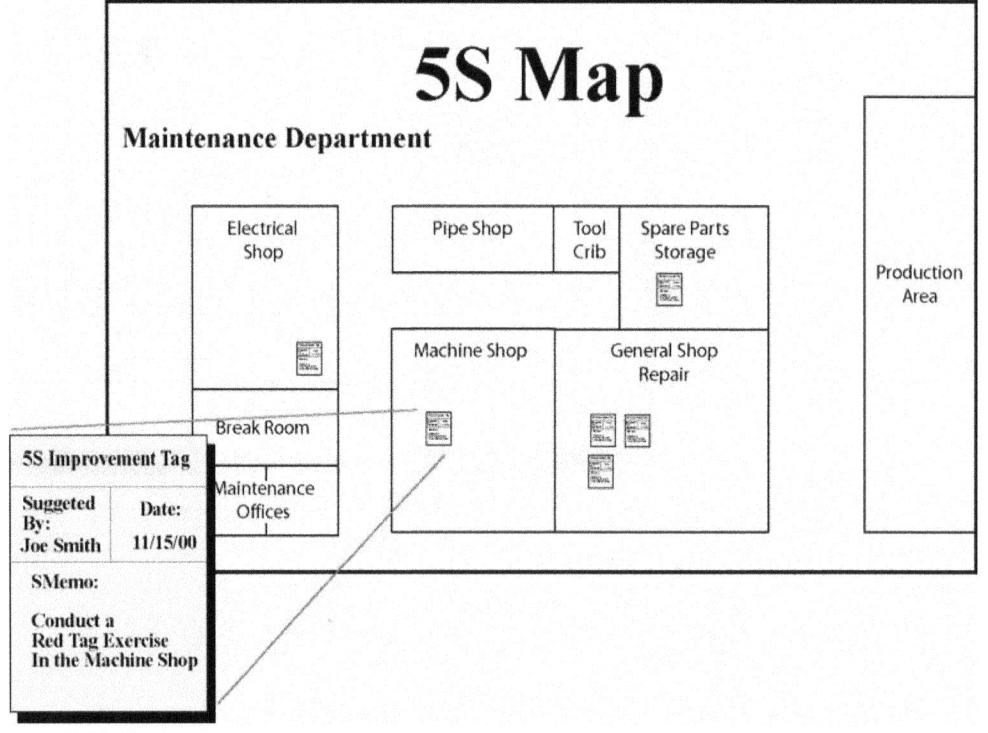

Planning & Implementing 5S

Make 5s Part of Daily Work

Introduction	If people carry out 3S maintenance activities only when they see conditions slipping, 5S implementation will not be effective. Maintenance must become a natural part of everyone's regular work duties.
Two Approaches	There are two approaches that help make 5S maintenance a part of the everyday work routine: • Visual 5S • Five-minute 5S.
Visual 5S	The visual approach makes the level of 5S conditions obvious at a glance. The key point is – anyone should be able to distinguish between normal and abnormal conditions at a glance.
Five-minute 5S	The term "Five-minute 5S" is a loose one, it can be six minutes or three or whatever. The point is to make the 3S work brief, effective, and habitual.

Planning & Implementing 5S

Auditing 3S Activities

Introduction

After the 3S jobs have been assigned and incorporated into everyday work routines, we still need to evaluate how well the 5S's are being maintained. This is accomplished by auditing the 5S activities. A useful tool for this is called the 5 Point Checklist.

The Five Point Checklist

The 5 Point Checklist is used to evaluate the standard clean up levels in terms of the 3S's. The check list uses a 5 point scale.

Five Point Checklist Procedure

Use the following procedure for completing a Five Point Checklist:

Step	Action
	Performing The Audit
1	Inspect the target area
2	Fill out the top section of the form by providing: • Name of the Target Area • Date of Inspection • The name of the person conducting the audit • Page number.
3	List all of the processes and inspection points under the "Process & Checkpoint" column.
4	Inspect the first process and checkpoint listed.
5	Circle the appropriate number in the "Organization Level" column. **Note:** *1 is low and 5 is high.*
6	Circle the appropriate number in the "Orderliness Level " column **Note:** *1 is low and 5 is high.*
7	Circle the appropriate number in the "Cleanliness Level " column **Note:** *1 is low and 5 is high.*

Continued on next page

Planning & Implementing 5S

Auditing 3S Activities, Continued

Five Point Checklist Procedure (continued)

Step	Action
8	Go to the next check point and repeat steps 5 through 7.
	Scoring The Audit
9	Add up the three scores for each checkpoint and place the total in the "Total" column.
10	Repeat the process for each checkpoint.
11	

If...	Then...
This is not the first audit	Enter the scores from the "Total" column of the previous audit in the "Prev. Total" Column.
This is the first Audit	Leave the "Prev. Total" Column blank.

Step	Action
12	Calculate the average totals for each of the three columns.
13	Calculate the sum of the totals in the "Total" column.
14	Calculate the sum of the totals in the "Prev. Total" column.

Figure 34: Example Five Point Checklist

The following is an example of a Five Point Checklist used in a plant:

Five-Pont Standardized Cleanup-level Checklist		Target Area		Date		Entered By:		Page	
No.	Process & Checkpoint	Organizational Level	Orderliness Level	Cleanliness Level	Total	Prev. Total
1		1 2 3 4 5	1 2 3 4 5	1 2 3 4 5		
2		1 2 3 4 5	1 2 3 4 5	1 2 3 4 5		
3		1 2 3 4 5	1 2 3 4 5	1 2 3 4 5		
4		1 2 3 4 5	1 2 3 4 5	1 2 3 4 5		
5		1 2 3 4 5	1 2 3 4 5	1 2 3 4 5		
6		1 2 3 4 5	1 2 3 4 5	1 2 3 4 5		
7		1 2 3 4 5	1 2 3 4 5	1 2 3 4 5		

Planning & Implementing 5S

Planning Our Future

Overview

Introduction

This Chapter provides the guidance required for effectively implementing the 5S program.

Purpose

The purpose of Planning Our Future is to provide a vision for a total implementation of the program across the entire operation.

In this Chapter

The topics described in this chapter are located as indicated below

Topic	See Page
Performance Improvement Implementation Plan	129
Changing 5S Roll Out Activities	137

Planning & Implementing 5S

Performance Improvement Implementation Plan

Overview

Introduction	This section describes the methodology for Implementing the program that you have designed.
Description	The implementation plan consists of the following • Performance improvement steering team structure • Performance improvement deployment plan • Announce upper management's decision to introduce the 5S program • Establish 5S policies and goals • Form a master plan for implementing the 5S program • Hold kick off.
Purpose	The purpose of the implementation plan is to provide a framework for carrying out the plans you have developed in this program.
In this Section	The topics described in this section are located as indicated below

Topic	See Page
5S Policies & Goals	132
Master Plan	134
Kick Off	136

Planning & Implementing 5S

5S Policies & Goals

Introduction This unit describes the methodology for establishing 5S policies & goals.

Description A sub team of the steering committee is established and given the responsibility establishing the 5S policies & goals for the entire facility.

Purpose The purpose is to ensure a common approach to implementing the 5S program.

Procedure Use the following procedure to implement:

Step	Action
1	Meet with the plant manager and develop a sub team charter defining your team's role and mission.
2	Review all of the materials you produced in the Planning & Implementing 5S workshop. Look at the methodology you learned for workplace analysis and the Changing The Workplace sections of the workshop.
3	Define a set of policy recommendations for each major activity and submit them to the plant manager for review and comment.
4	Establish a set of recommended goals complete with time lines for completion of each. Submit these recommendations to the plant manager for review and comment.
5	Meet with the plant manager to make corrections and additions to the policies and guidelines.
6	Plant manager approves and issues the policies and goals.

Planning & Implementing 5S

Master Plan

Introduction   This unit describes the methodology for defining the master plan.

Description   The master plan defines how the program will be carried out in detail. It defines the work to be accomplished, established a schedule, assigns resources, establishes a budget, and assigns accountabilities,

Purpose   The purpose of the master plan is to provide a comprehensive plan for accomplishing the goals for implementing and sustaining the 5S program. Major headings of the plan include:
- Breakdown of tasks and activities
- Time schedule for initiation and completion of defined tasks and activities
- Estimated resource requirements
- Defined roles and responsibilities for steering team members and other participants
- Accountabilities and standards of performance for each team member.

Continued on next page

Planning & Implementing 5S

Master Plan, Continued

Procedure   Use the following procedure to implement

Step	Action
1	Review the deployment plan; this will become the basis of your Master Plan.
2	Conduct a brainstorming session to identify and agree upon all tasks required to implement the 5S program in your facility.
3	Develop a time schedule for each activity and put it in a network diagram and a Gantt Chart. (Microsoft project is an excellent tool for this purpose.)
4	Estimate the resources required for each task or activity.
5	Define the roles of each team member and assign tasks to each member.
6	Assign accountabilities for tasks and define the standards of performance for each team member.

Planning & Implementing 5S

Kick Off

Introduction   This unit describes the methodology for the kick off of the 5S program for the rest of the organization.

Description   The kick off consists of a formal celebration, in which the purpose of the process is announced to the outside world (Customer and suppliers) as well as plant employees. It is different from upper management's decision to introduce the 5S program because it is a public announcement coupled with a celebration.

Purpose   The purpose is to symbolize a new beginning in which historical thought patterns, practices, and paradigms are challenged. Management effectively drives a stake in the ground in announcing a new way of conducting business.

Procedure   Use the following procedure to implement:

Step	Action
1	Establish a kick off sub team in the steering committee.
2	Meet with the plant manager to define goals and activities.
3	Establish a budget for the kick off.
4	Determine the activities that will be involved, time frames, and cost limits, and assign each member the responsibility for one or more activity.
5	Schedule the kick off and select a rain date.
	Prepare announcements and press releases.
6	Conduct the 5S kick off.

136

Planning & Implementing 5S

5S Roll-Out Activities

Overview

Introduction

This section describes the various activities that other organizations have used to sustain the principles and practices taught in this workshop.

Purpose

The purpose of providing examples of activities is to make it easier for the steering team to come up with their own unique program based on best practices.

In this Section

The topic described in this section is located as indicated below:

Topic	See Page
Tools and Techniques to Sustain 5S	138

137

Planning & Implementing 5S

Tools and Techniques to Sustain Workplace Organization

Introduction

A common cry from plant managers, operations managers, and supervisors is; "No matter how hard we try to maintain the 5S program, things always seem to go back to the way they were." 5S isn't a once and done type of thing, as we pointed out earlier, you have to work at it to sustain it.

Purpose

All jobs are easier if you have the correct tools. This page is intended to provide you with several tools that will help you sustain the program. You have to tailor your toolbox to fit your organization.

Continued on next page

Planning & Implementing 5S

Tools and Techniques to Sustain Workplace Organization,
Continued

Tools

The following tools have proved to be effective in sustaining 5S efforts:

Tool	Description
Slogans	Slogans vary and they need to come from your workforce through employee suggestion. They can be displayed on posters, buttons, stickers, and other types of displays. They should be kept simple and appropriate for all audiences.
Posters	Posters are useful and can be made with a minimum amount of material cost. They should be neatly done and well thought out to support the theme of 5S. Sloppy posters will do more harm than good. Put up new posters every six months or so.
Photo exhibits and storyboards	A member of the implementation team searches the workplace for good and bad examples of 5S implementation. Photos are placed on a storyboard and posted in a high traffic area such as the time clock, cafeteria, entrance ways, etc.
Newsletters	One of the most effective tools is a 5S Newsletter. It contains articles on factory conditions, activities, and implementation tips. Employees are given recognition for contributions and successes. You will find that many people actually look forward to the next edition.
Maps	5S Maps show the workplace layout. Their purpose is to clarify who is responsible for a particular area or the workplace. They are displayed in a high traffic area in the particular workspace area. A supply of improvement tags is made available for use by anyone who notices something that needs improvement in the area.

Appendix

Topic	See Page
Example Documents	143
Forms	151

Example Documents

Form	See Page
Sample Commissioning Letter	144
One Point Lesson Example	146
5 Why Analysis Example	147
5S Procedure Example	148

Planning & Implementing 5S

Sample Commissioning Letter

MEMORANDUM

To: All Plant Personnel
From: John Jacobson Plant Manager
Date: June 24, 2010
Subject: Implementation of 5S at our facility
Effective Date: July 1, 201065

The plant management team has made the decision to implement 5S in our facility. 5S is a Japanese tool for workplace, office and shop floor improvement. It is also regarded as good housekeeping tool. This tool is combination of five words and every word contains S as first letter:
1. Sort - Determine what is needed and not needed for efficient production and remove unneeded items
2. Set In Order - Organize what is left
3. Shine - A system of inspection and cleaning
4. Standardize - Making sure that the p[program is carried out the same way through out the organization
5. Sustain - ensuring that the program continues to function properly and not become another "flavor of the month".

The 5S philosophy is focused for improving our processes, reducing wastes, saving time, providing you a safe and healthy environment.

Expectations

The management team expects the following to occurs as a result of implementing this program:
- Overall factory productivity is the most important expectation of the management team. . We expect to see a 15% increase by 7/1/2011
- Reduction in time spent looking for tools and materials is critical to the success of this project. . We expect to see a reduction of 20% by 1/15/2011
- Spending on replacing lost or damaged items has been increasing over the past two years.. We expect to see a 20% reduction in spending by 7/1/2011
- Workspace house keeping has been deteriorating over the past three years.. We expect to see 100% compliance in the application of Shine procedures by target area personnel by 10/1/2010

Planning & Implementing 5S

Scope of the 5S Project

The 5S project will be implemented across the entire facility. The management team has selected eight (8) target areas and has set the priorities for implementation of the 5S Program in these target areas as follows:

Target Area:	Priority:
Maintenance Department	1
Mixing	2
Bakeshop	3
Packaging	4
Shipping Warehouse	5
Receiving Warehouse	6
Office Area	7
QC Laboratory	8

5S Champion

The 5S Champion will be Edward Vanderhoof, Assistant Plant Manager. Mr. Edward Vanderhoof is accountable for the success or failure of the project. He will be responsible for making key project decisions, which are outside the approved boundaries for the 5S team. I expect him to ensure that the 5S project is given All of the management backing it requires.

5S Team Leader

The team leader for the 5S Project will be Andrea Metcalf. Ms. Metcalf will be responsible for:

- Assisting in the initial audit and writing of the team charter
- Selecting the 5S team members with the guidance of the 5S Champion and management
- Ensuring that a participative approach is taken to all 5S implementation
- Providing direction and support to the 5S team
- Preparing agendas and make decisions at 5S team meetings
- Obtaining the resources needed by the 5S team
- Ensuring that the 5S process is applied systematically
- Reporting to management on a regular basis.

I expect and require all managers and personnel to cooperate with the 5S project team and follow the 5S implementation plan once it is approved. If you have any questions about this program, please contact your manager, Andrea Metcalf, or Edward Vanderhoof.

One Point Lesson Example

One-Point Lesson

☐ 1. Basic Knowledge
☐ 2. Problem Case Study
☒ 3. Improvement Case Study
(Check One)

Theme:

Current Problem:

Mechanic has to place the block on the main rail and tighten the locking bolts while holding it in place. The mechanic has to hold the block in place while using the socket wrench. He/she can not support thier body because both hands are tied up, results in strain injuries.

Descriptions of Improvement

Change the blocks to lever action grips that do not require tightening with a wreench

Results

Strain injuries have been reduced by 65%
Time required to block the crane is recuded from 15 minutes to 4 minutes

Written By: _____ Reference #: _____
Location: _____ Revision #: _____
Date: _____ Revision Date: _____

Planning & Implementing 5S

5 Why Analysis Example

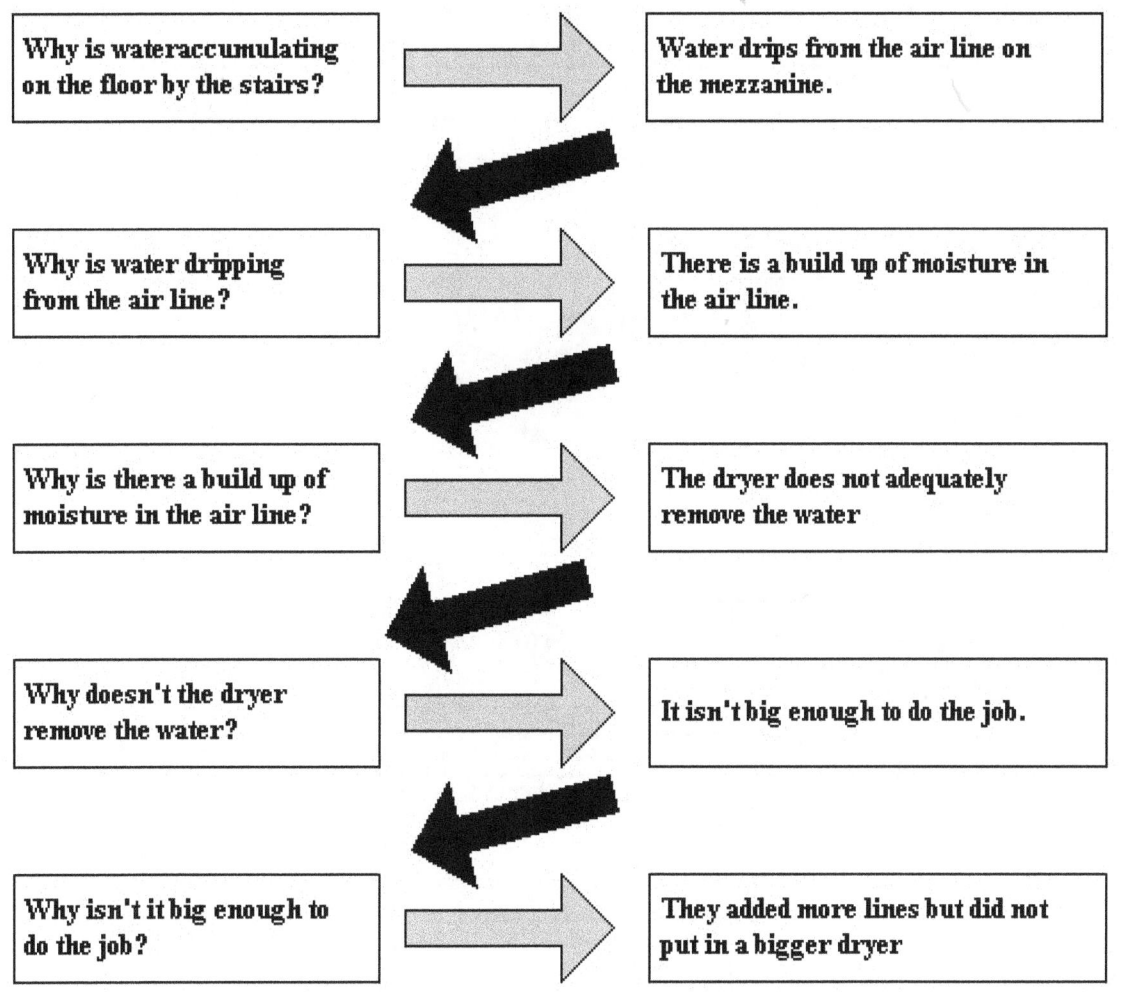

Planning & Implementing 5S

5S Procedure Example

Company Facility	**5S Procedure** Red Tagging	Proc No 5006-01 Section 1.0 Effective Date

Scope: This procedure provides the general guidelines for conducting a red tagging exercise. This procedure does not supersede, nor does it relieve responsibility for compliance with any other procedure(s) that may be required.

Purpose The purpose of red tagging is to
- Visually identify unneeded items
- Identify why the items is not needed
- Who identified the problem

**Tool &
Equipments:**
- Red Tags
- Tape

**Performing
Red Tagging** Use the following steps to perform this procedure:

Step	Action	
	Inspect Target Area	
1	Visually inspect the target area using the red tagging inspection sheet.	
2	Determine need	

If...	Then...
The item is needed for production	Keep item in target area
The item is not needed for production	Apply red tag
The item is not needed in quantity present	Apply red tag to quantity not needed
The item is needed infrequently	Apply red tag

Continued on next page

Rev 0, 3/2006   1 of 3

Planning & Implementing 5S

Company Facility	5S Procedure Red Tagging	Proc No SOP 01 Sheet of 8 Effective Date

Performing Red Tagging (continued)

Step	Action
	Filling out the Red tag
3	Fill out the red tag, provide the following information: • Red Tag Number (next number on log) • The unneeded item • Date • Quantity • Reason for red tagging • Category. •
4	Enter the item in the Unneeded Items log, provide the following information: • Unneeded Item • Tag Number • Reason for Tagging
5	Hang the tag on the unneeded item.
6	Go to next item.
	Removal
7	Remove all red tagged items to the Red Tag Holding Area.
	Disposition
8	Decide what to do with each item using the Item Disposition List.
9	Dispose of items according to the Item Disposition List.

Continued on next page

Company Facility	5S Procedure Red Tagging	Proc No SO001 Sec of 1 0 Effective Date

Figure 1:
Red Tag

Red Tag No: _____

Unneeded Item: _____
Tagger Name: _____ Date: _____
Target Area: _____
Quantity: _____
Reason For Red Tag: _____

Category: _____
Disposition: _____

APPROVAL

This procedure was approved for use by:

Approved by: _____ _____ _____
                         Name   Title   Date

Approved by: _____ _____ _____
                         Name   Title   Date

Approved by: _____ _____ _____
                         Name   Title   Date

Forms

5S Team Charter

5S Team Charter

Purpose:

Directions:

Today's Date	Target Area:
5S Champion:	Target Area Supervisor:

Team Member Roles: Names:

Team Facilitator

Team Leader

Recorder/Reporter

Other Members:

152

Planning & Implementing 5S

5S Team Charter

Purpose of Target Area

Functions of Target Area

Problem Statement (Why was this chosen? Summarize current problems)

Vision (Describe how you want the target area to be.)

Guidelines, Restrictions and Boundaries for the project

Other information/Notes

Planning & Implementing 5S

Action Plan

Team Name: _____ Team Leader: _____

Directions:	1.	Brainstorm and identify all action items
	2.	Decide the sequence of actions
	3.	For each action, decide who is responsible, the completion date, and how it will be accomplished
	4.	Use the document to monitor your progress.

Action	Who	By When	How

Planning & Implementing 5S

Process Charting Symbols

Symbol	Description	Example
Start and end symbols	Represented as circles, ovals or rounded rectangles, usually containing the word "Start" or "End", or another phrase signaling the start or end of a process.	
Arrow	An arrow coming from one symbol and ending at another symbol represents that control passes to the symbol the arrow points to.	
Processing steps	Represented as rectangles (or oblongs)	
Input/Output	Represented as a parallelogram	
Conditional or decision	Represented as a diamond (rhombus). These typically contain a Yes/No question or True/False test. This symbol is unique in that it has two arrows coming out of it, usually from the bottom point and right point, one corresponding to Yes or True, and one corresponding to No or False. The arrows should always be labeled.	
Document	Represented as a rectangle with a wavy base;	
Manual operation	Represented by a trapezoid with the longest parallel side at the top, to represent an operation or adjustment to process that can only be made manually.	

Planning & Implementing 5S

Responsibility Matrix Form

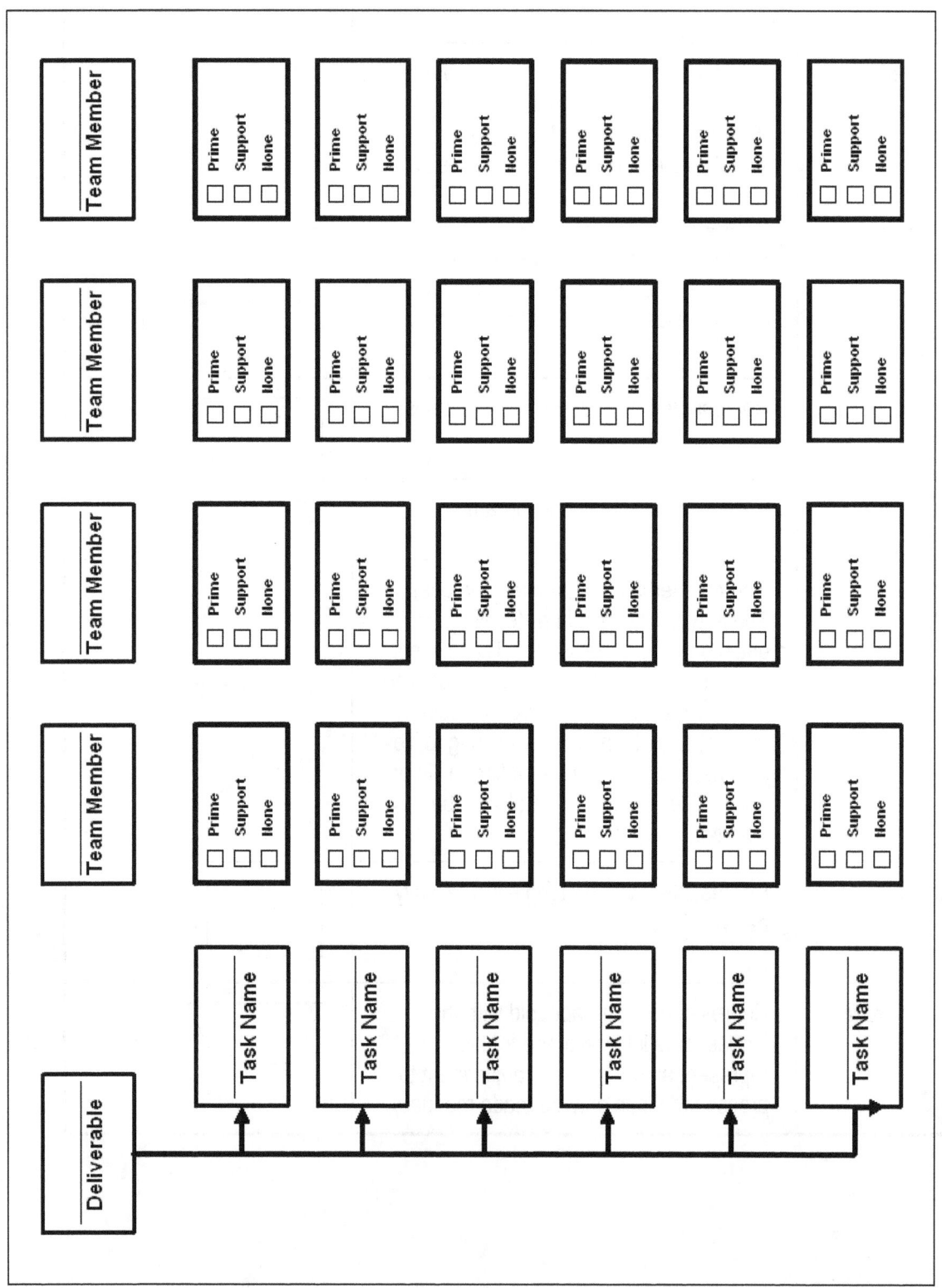

Planning & Implementing 5S

VFA Scoring Guide

Evaluation Point / Activity	1	2	3	4	5	Ideal Condition
Sort needed & unneeded items	Items still unsorted	Only a few items have been sorted	Some (but not most) items have been sorted	Most items have been sorted	All items sorted and in needed & unneeded groups	Items which are needed & unneeded are easily recognized
Dispose of unneeded items	No items disposed of	Only a few items disposed of	Some (but not all) items disposed of	Nearly all items disposed of	All unneeded items removed & needed items organized	Only needed items remain in workspace
Store needed items	Items randomly inserted into storage spaces	Items in storage area beginning to look organized	Items in storage area are generally organized	Most items stored so that they can be seen & easily retrieved	All items stored so that they can be seen & easily retrieved	All items stored and can be found easily
Eliminate waste space	No idea about where space is being wasted	Some storage shelves added to empty space	More storage shelves added	Key storage areas have been optimized	Almost all storage areas have been optimized	Wasted space eliminated & workspace more spacious
Eliminate searching waste	Storage space does not follow the "wide & shallow" rule	Learned about search waste & started to prevent it	People have begun to notice & eliminate search waste	Most but not all search waste eliminated	All search waste eliminated	All items stored neatly and visible to eliminate searching
Eliminate walking waste	No idea of how much walking waste is in workspace	Learned about motion waste & started to prevent it	People have begun to notice & eliminate walking waste	Most but not all walking waste eliminated	All walking waste eliminated	Principles of motion economy are implemented
Eliminate excess inventory or piles	There are piles of inventory all over workspace	Have started to eliminate excess inventory	Made obvious progress eliminating excess inventory	Have eliminated most of the excess inventory	All excess inventory is gone and prevention steps in place	No excess inventory and no place to put it
Create visual workplace	Can't tell where things belong by simply looking	Can't tell where a few things belong by simply looking	Considerable progress made in visible work place	Can tell where most things belong by simply looking	Can tell where almost everything belongs by simply looking	Signs, labels, color codes, etc. in full use

Planning & Implementing 5S

VFA Problem Chart

Workplace Problem Chart

PART: _____ WORKPLACE/TEAMS: _____

	If you think it is a problem, photograph it.		Like a mirror, VFP shows everything— good and bad.		Do a careful, thorough search for problems.		Get a clear focus.

Planning & Implementing 5S

VFA Feedback Chart

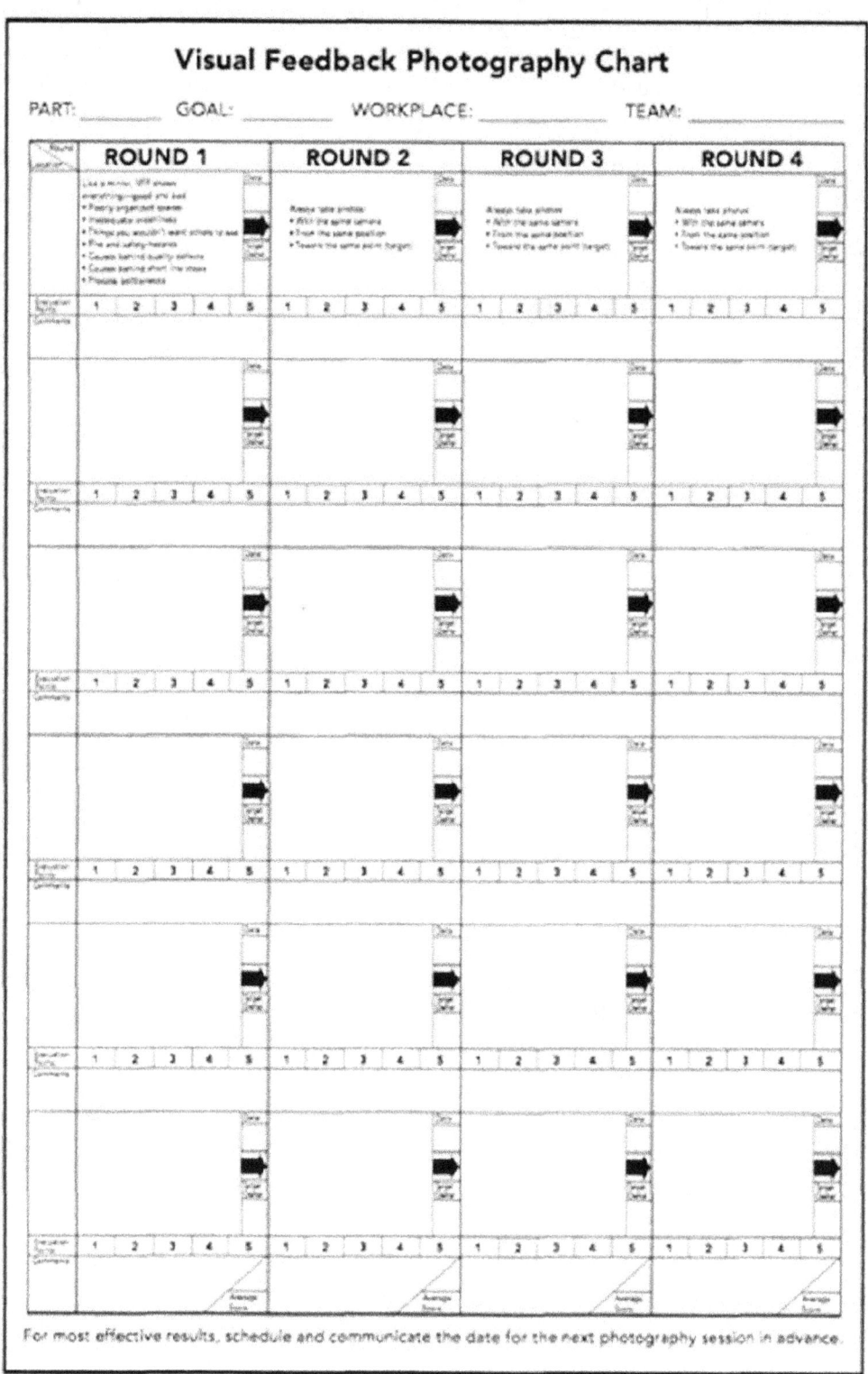

How To Create VFA Forms

Introduction

The best way to create either a VFA Problem Chart or a VFA Photography chart is to create them use AutoCAD (or equivalent) and printing them out on a plotter or large format printer.

Figure 35: VFA Problem Chart Block

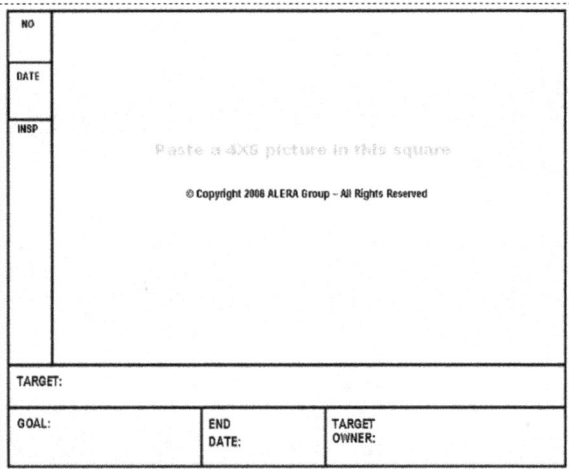

Chart Drawing Procedure

Use the following procedure to create a VFA Problem Chart:

Step	Action
1	Set the page size to 3' X 4', Portrait. Set the margins as follows: 1. Top ....3" 1. Bottom ....1" 2. Left Side ....2" 3. Right side.......2".
2	Starting on the left side of the page 3, draw a box 8" W X 10" H.
3	Make a box 2" W X 6" H in the upper left corner as shown in Figure 35'.
4	Make two 2"W 1" H boxes and Insert the word "Insert the words "NO." and "DATE" and place then inside the box created in step 3. Insert the work "INSP" in the remaining space in the box created in step 3.
5	Make another box 8" W X 1" H and place it below box created in step 3 as shown. Insert the word "TARGET:" in the box as shown in Figure 35.
6	Create a Box 8" W X 3" H and place it below the box created in step 5 as shown.

Continued on next page

Chart Drawing Procedure, Continued

Step	Action
7	Create a 2 boxes 3"W X 3"H. Insert the words "GOAL:" and "TARGET OWNER" as shown in Figure 35. Insert the word "END DATE" in the remaining space.
8	Copy the box and paste in next to the first. Paste two more copies next to the previous box until you have 4 boxes across the top. Group these 4 boxes together and copy the grouped boxes.
9	Paste 3 rows of grouped boxes below the top row.
10	Insert the word "COMMENTS" ¼ inch below the last group of boxes.

Figure 36: VFA Photography Chart Block

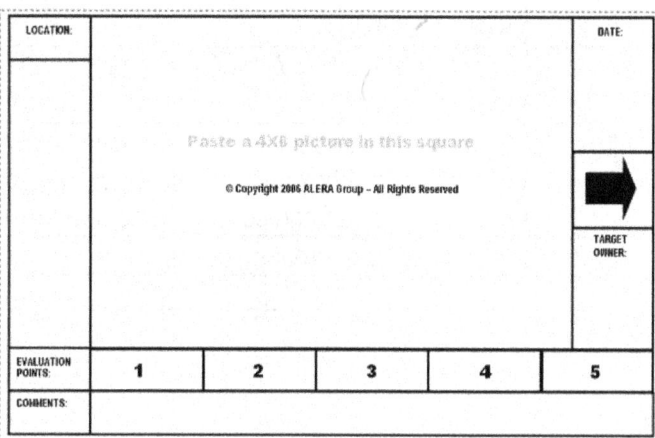

Chart Drawing Procedure

Use the following procedure to create a VFA Photography Chart

Step	Action
1	Set the page size to 3' X 4', Portrait. Set the margins as follows: 2. Top ....3" 4. Bottom ....1" 5. Left Side ....2" 6. Right side........2"
2	Starting on the left side of the page 3, draw a box 8" W X 10" H
3	Make a box 1" W X 6" H in the upper left corner as shown in Figure 36. Insert the word "LOCATION" as shown
4	Make another box 1" W X 6" H in the upper right corner of the box created in step 2 as shown in Figure 36. Insert the word "LOCATION" as shown

161

Planning & Implementing 5S

Chart Drawing Procedure, Continued

Step	Action
5	Create box 1"W X 2" H. Draw a black arrow pointed to the right as shown in Figure 36. Place this box in the box created in step 4 so that it is four inches from the top.
6	In the upper portion of the box created in step 4, place the word "DATE" and below the box created in step 5 place the word "TARGET OWNER" as shown in Figure 36.
7	Create a box 1" X1" and place it below box created in step 4. Insert the words "EVALUATION POINTS" as shown in Figure 36.
8	Create 5 boxes 1.4" W 1" H, insert the Numbers 1 through 5 and place them next to the box created in step 7.
9	Create a box 1" X1" and place it below box created in step 7. Insert the word "COMMENTS".
10	Create another box 7" W X 1" H and place it next to the box created in step 9.
11	Copy the box and paste in next to the first. Paste two more copies next to the previous box until you have 4 boxes across the top. Group these 4 boxes together and copy the grouped boxes.
12	Paste 3 rows of grouped boxes below the top row.

Planning & Implementing 5S

Workplace Scan Checklist

Target Area: _____

Category	Item	Date Rated	Ratings				
Sort	Distinguish between what is needed and not needed						
	Unneeded equipment, tools, furniture, etc. are present						
	Unneeded items are on walls, bulletin boards, etc.						
	Items are present in aisle ways, stairways, corners, etc.						
	Unneeded inventory, supplies, parts, or materials are present						
	Safety hazards exist						
Set In Order	A place for everything and everything in its place						
	Correct places for items are not obvious						
	Items are not in their correct places						
	Aisle ways workstations, equipment locations are not indicated						
	Items are not put away immediately after use						
	Height and quantity limits are not obvious						
Shine	Cleaning, and looking for ways to keep it clean and organized						
	Floors, walls, stairs, and surfaces are not free of dirt, oil, and grease						
	Equipment is not kept clean and free of dirt, oil, and grease						
	Cleaning materials are not easily accessible						
	Lines, labels, signs, etc. are not clean and unbroken						
	Other cleaning problems (of any kind) are present						
Standardize	Maintain and Monitor the first three categories						
	Necessary information not visible						
	All standards are not known and visible						
	Checklists don't exist for all cleaning and maintenance jobs						
	All quantities and limits are not easily recognizable						
	How many items can't be located in 30 seconds?						
Sustain	Stick to the rules						
	How many workers have not had 5S training?						
	How many times was 5S not performed last week?						
	Number of times that personal belongings are not neatly stored						
	Number of times job aids are not available or up to date						
	Number of times daily 5S inspections were not performed last week						

Planning & Implementing 5S

Red Tag Inspection Sheet

Target Area: _____

Purpose	To ensure that the team examine all items for Red–Tagging
Directions	1. Examine all items under each category
	2. When an item does not belong, attach a red–tag
	3. Enter a check when an item is inspected

Search the following places
- Aisles ☐
- Cabinets and drawers ☐
- Floors ☐
- Offices ☐
- Operation Areas ☐
- Other storage places ☐
- Racks ☐
- Shelves ☐
- Small Rooms ☐
- Under Stairways ☐
- Work Stations ☐

Search walls and boards
- Bulletin boards ☐
- Items hung on walls ☐
- Signboards ☐
- Other items ☐

Search for unneeded equipment
- Portable equipment ☐
- Machines ☐
- Transport equipment ☐
- Electrical equipment ☐
- Wire, fixtures, etc. ☐
- Plumbing I pipefitting equipment ☐
- Pipes, hoses, etc. ☐
- Tools ☐
☐

Search for unneeded furniture
- Benches and work tables ☐
- Cabinets ☐
- Carts ☐
- Chairs ☐
- Other furniture ☐

Search for unneeded Materials/supplies
- Finished product ☐
- Parts ☐
- Raw materials ☐
- Supplies ☐
- Work in progress ☐

Search for other unneeded items
- Bump caps, hard hats, etc ☐
- Portable containers ☐
- Trash cans ☐
- Work clothes ☐
- Work shoes ☐
☐
☐
☐
☐
☐
☐
☐
☐

Planning & Implementing 5S

Unneeded Items Log

Target Area: _____

Unneeded Item	#	Date	Reason For Red–Tagging	Disposition

Planning & Implementing 5S

Item Disposition List

Purpose	To help the team decide what to do with Red–Tagged items
Directions	1. For each item, determine the proper category
	2. Determine the action to be taken
	3. Disposition item.

Category	Action To Be Taken
Obsolete	■ Sell ■ Hold for depreciation ■ Give away ■ Throw away
Defective	■ Return to supplier ■ Throw away
Scrap	■ Remove from area
Trash	■ Throw away ■ Recycle
Unneeded in this area	■ Remove from area – send to appropriate area
Used at least once per day	■ Store in area
Used once per week	■ Store in close accessible location
Used once per month	■ Store in where accessible in plant
Seldom used	■ Store in distant place ■ Sell ■ Give away ■ Throw away
Use Unknown	■ Determine use ■ Remove to appropriate location

166

Planning & Implementing 5S

Set In Order Inspection Sheet

Purpose	To ensure that the team examine all items for Set In Order
Directions	1. Examine all items under each category
	2. When an item does not belong, attach a red–tag
	3. Enter a check when an item is inspected

Equipment
Portable equipment ☐
Machines ☐
Transport equipment ☐
Electrical equipment ☐
Wire, fixtures, etc. ☐
Plumbing I pipefitting equipment ☐
Pipes, hoses, etc. ☐
Tools ☐

Furniture
Benches and work tables ☐
Cabinets ☐
Carts ☐
Chairs ☐
Other furniture ☐

Materials/Supply/Inventory
Finished product ☐
Parts ☐
Raw materials ☐
Supplies ☐
Work in progress ☐

Other Items
Bump caps, hard hats, etc ☐
Portable containers ☐
Trash cans ☐
Work clothes ☐
Work shoes ☐

Planning & Implementing 5S

Shine Inspection Sheet

Purpose	To ensure that the team examine all items for Shine
Directions	1. Examine all items under each category
	2. When an item does not belong, attach a red–tag
	3. Enter a check when an item is inspected

Large Surfaces		Surfaces Of Equipment And Furniture	
Aisles	☐	Portable equipment	☐
Cabinets and drawers	☐	Machines	☐
Floors	☐	Transport equipment	☐
Offices	☐	Electrical equipment	☐
Operation Areas	☐	Wire, fixtures, etc.	☐
Other storage places	☐	Plumbing I pipefitting equipment	☐
Racks	☐	Pipes, hoses, etc.	☐
Shelves	☐	Tools	☐
Small Rooms	☐		
Under Stairways	☐	**Other**	
Work Stations	☐	Materials & Supplies	☐
		Trash cans	☐
Inside Equipment		Bulletin boards	☐
Machines	☐	Labels & signs	☐
Transport equipment, conveyors	☐	Small tools	☐
Closets	☐	Hoses, cords, tubing, etc	☐
Drawers	☐	Other items	☐
cabinets	☐		
Sheds	☐		
Tool boxes	☐		
	☐		

Planning & Implementing 5S

Initial Cleaning Plan

Team Name: _____ Team Leader: _____

| Directions: | 1. Brainstorm and identify all action items
2. Decide the sequence of actions
3. For each action, decide who is responsible, the completion date, and how it will be accomplished
4. Use the document to monitor your progress. | | |

Action	Who	By When	How

Planning & Implementing 5S

Standardize Planning Worksheet

Team Name: _____   Team Leader: _____

Directions:
1. Enter the name of the Target area in the space above
2. Determine the tasks and where they should be completed and enter information in to the appropriate column
3. Determine who should be responsible for performing it and by when and enter information in to the appropriate column
4. Decide how and when it should be performed and enter information in to the appropriate column

Action	Where	Who	By When	How

Planning & Implementing 5S

Sustain Planning Worksheet

Team Name: _____ Team Leader: _____

Purpose	To help the team to sustain the 5S standards and guidelines
Directions:	1. Enter the name of the Target area in the space above
	2. Determine from whom the adherence to the 5S standard and guidelines and procedures is necessary and enter information in to the appropriate column
	3. Determine the method you will use to ensure compliance and enter information in to the appropriate column
	4. Determine when it must be accomplished and enter information in to the appropriate column

Who	Standard, Guidelines, Procedures	Method	When

Planning & Implementing 5S

Resources

Topic	See Page
Books	174
Training Programs	178
Services	179
5S Blog	181

ALERA Group Website

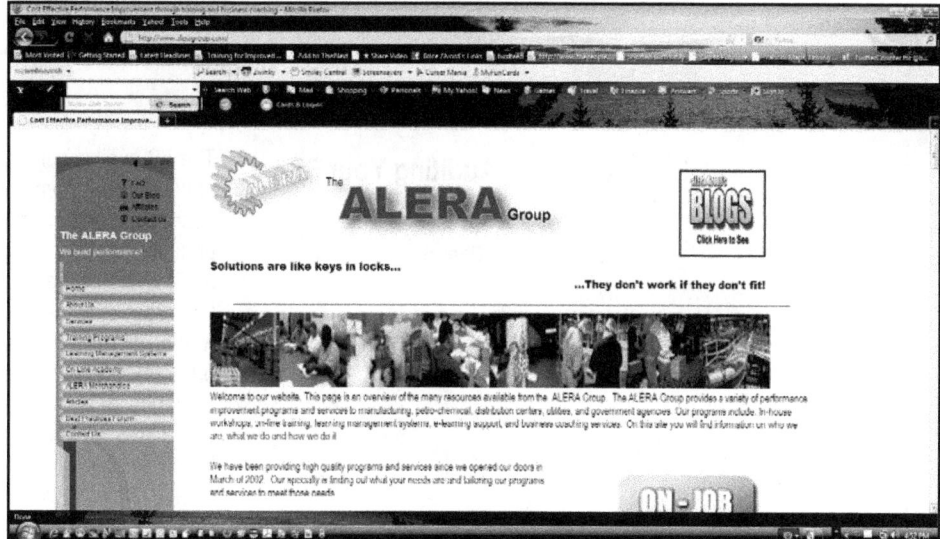

http://www.aleragroup.com

Planning & Implementing 5S

Books From ALERA Publishing Group

Planning & Implementing 5S

Paperback	$24.99
Hard Cover	$36.53

The Planning & Implementing 5S program shows you how to organize a Performance Improvement Steering Team, how to analyze the workplace, how to plan a facility-wide improvement program, and how to sustain your efforts.

The 5S workbook is the companion to Planning and Implementing 5S by Brice Alvord. It provides the tools used in the ALERA workshop.

5S Workbook

Paperback	$14.48

Auditing Your 5S Program

Paperback	$14.99

The 5S audit is critical to the success of your 5S program. It is often overlooked or considered an unnecessary extra expense. The audit validates the accountability of the target area owners for complying with 5S plans. Without the audit, the program slowly withers away and becomes ineffective. A close look at 5S failures will reveal a lack of or an ineffective auditing program. This book explains how to conduct a proper 5S audit.

Building A 5Steam

Paperback	$17.99

Building A 5S team explains what a 5S Team needs to know in order to function properly. This book covers how to form a team, write a charter, how to run the team once it is created. this book provides a foundation for teamwork and continuous improvement activities.

Strategic Planning For 5S

Paperback	$30.51

Strategic Planning for 5S is intended for managers and steering committee members who are considering the implementation of a 5S program. It shows how to apply Strategic Thinking to the 5S planning and implementation process and develop a strong business case for change

Continued on next page

Planning & Implementing 5S

Books From ALERA Publishing Group, Continued

Advanced 5S Implementation Media Files

CD: $18.99

The Form Tools CD contains a variety of 5S implementation forms and job aids in either MS Word or Excel formats. These forms can be modified as you see fit to meet the specific needs of your 5S program. This is the perfect companion to Advanced 5S Implementation.

Training

How to Train People On The Job

Paperback $18.53

Performance Based Training

Paperback $21.95

NEW and REVISED workbook for Training On the Job Trainers. Covers adult learning theory, why shadow training does not work, how to perform a simple job/task analysis, how to develop trainer's guides and teach using the Four Step Method This book is intended as a guide to Performance Based Instructional Design. It covers how to conduct an effective Training Analysis including Job/Task Analysis, how to identify and define realistic competencies and instructional objectives and how to organize analysis data into a performance based training design. The book also explains how to develop important training documents including trainer's guides and lesson plans, participant manuals, and support materials including training and job aids and other media. Performance Based Training: Building a Competent Workforce is intended for the training professional as well as those people who have been given a training assignment. It is also a good reference for managers and supervisors to help them build a stronger workforce and to support company training efforts.

Continued on next page

Books From ALERA Publishing Group, Continued

Advanced Instructional Design

Paperback $21.95

Advanced Instructional design focuses on the steps required to develop a performance based training design. Chapters include information conducting a Job Task Analysis and the Design of the training program. Other topics include defining competencies, conducting a DACUM, writing performance based objectives, developing criterion tests, Sequencing training elements, and writing a training blueprint. This book does not cover the development of training materials that will be addressed in another book yet to be published.

Training, Continued

One Point Lessons

Paperback $11.94

This book is a training workbook for developing One-Point Lessons. It is designed to provide clear and simple explanations of procedures and techniques to quickly create short, cost effective training materials.

Operations Performance Improvement

Paperback $21.59
Hard Cover $36.30

Fundamentals of Operations Performance Analysis shows your OPI team how to develop effective solutions to persistent performance problems. Your team will learn how to isolate and understand the root cause of defects and failures within equipment mechanisms and peripheral systems. They will learn how to apply a systematic approach for effectively controlling those causes.

Overall Equipment Effectiveness

Paperback $17.56

Overall Equipment Effectiveness (OEE) is a universal measurement that has been used worldwide for over 10 years. It is a formula to measure the efficiency of production line equipment. In short, OEE measures the ratio of first-pass acceptable product actually produced to the theoretical amount that could be produced under optimal conditions.

Continued on next page

Planning & Implementing 5S

Books From ALERA Publishing Group, Continued

Strategic Thinking

Paperback $13.16

Strategic Thinking for Operations & Projects focuses on how to build a strategic based business case for change. It is a powerful communications tool for getting projects approved.

Fundamentals of Project Management

Paperback $16.38

Project Management Fundamentals covers the fundamental skills required to plan and implement project. It is intended for new project managers and managers with little or no project management experience.

Planning & Implementing 5S

Training Programs From ALERA Group

How To Train People On The Job

A 2 Day Hands-on Workshop that teaches your participants how to conduct On Job Training using the Four Step Method of Instruction.

Planning & Implementing 5S Workshop

A 3 Day Hands-On Workshop that teaches your participants how to plan and implement a basic 5S program. They will actually begin implementing 5S in a target area of your facility.

Team Based Problem Solving

A 2 Day Hands-on Workshop to teach your teams how to work together to identify and solve real problems in the workplace. Teams will address n actual problem and apply the tools to solve it.

Project Management Workshop

A 2 Day Hands-on Workshop that teaches the fundamentals of project management. Participants develop all of the elements of a project.

Overall Equipment Effectiveness

A 1 Day Hands-on Workshop to teach your participants what Overall Equipment Effectiveness is and how to calculate it accurately.

Try Z Seminar

A 2 ½ to 4 Day Hands-on Workshop from QCDSM Systems, Inc. See QCDSM Program Information on page **Error! Bookmark not defined.**.

178

Planning & Implementing 5S

Services From ALERA Group

Introduction	The ALERA Consulting Group exists to assist you in improving all areas of performance in your organization. We have a variety of state of the art tools and processes to help you identify performance needs and relate them to business practices and strategies.
Strategic Thinking	ALERA helps you develop strategic thinking in your organization; We conduct a strategic thinking workshop for selected members of your management team. We coach them through the application of the Strategic Thinking model to help them develop comprehensive and effective business cases for change within your organization.
Team Building	ALERA helps you design and deliver the right customized team development program, team building event, corporate retreat, or executive retreat that will improve your team's effectiveness, collaboration skills, and team-based results.
New Leader Assimilation	ALERA's Leader Assimilation program is based on the process designed by Kaiser Aluminum. Kaiser discovered that it normally took an incoming manager six months to become fully productive. The process was designed to reduce this amount of organizational down-time.
High Impact Change Management	ALERA's High Impact Change Management is a 3 phase organizational design program that assesses the organization with a performance audit, rationalizes change, and develops a comprehensive design. ALERA provides: design team formation and training, strategy focused design, alignment of the organization for maximum effectiveness, and building an empowered organization.
Asset Effectiveness (Focused Equipment Improvement)	ALERA helps your Operations Improvement Team develop the skills to address chronic equipment problems that hinder your profitability and overall performance. We provide workshops o help your team succeed. We evaluate your team's performance and coach individual members and your management team.

Continued on next page

Planning & Implementing 5S

Services From ALERA Group, Continued

Training Analysis	ALERA conducts or teaches your team to conduct a variety of training analysis including: training needs analysis, job/task analysis, cost benefit analysis, Our training professionals conduct training effectiveness audits, subject matter interviews, and individual performance evaluations.
Workplace Organization (5S planning and implementation)	ALERA helps you analyze your needs, design a program, plan 5S implementation, evaluate the progress of your program, perform 5S audits, coach your management team on implementation problems and opportunities.
Project Management	ALERA has experienced project managers who can assist you with keeping your performance improvement project or training project on schedule and under budget. We address your organizational needs and support consulting efforts with comprehensive training programs for your team as needed.
Technical Writing and Instructional Design and Development	ALERA can provide you with technical writers to help you develop standard operating procedures, lockout/tagout procedures technical documentation, training manuals, detailed process sheets.

180

Planning & Implementing 5S

Our Blogs

Improving Your Workplace

http://5sfundamentals.blogspot.com/

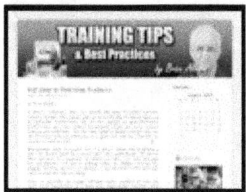

Training Tips & Best Practices

http://aleratraining.wordpress.com/

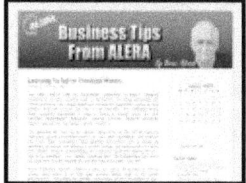

Business Tips from ALERA

http://goalera.wordpress.com/

Planning & Implementing 5S

Planning & Implementing 5S